Being Pure

THE PRACTICE OF VAJRASATTVA

Ringu Tulku Rinpoche

Compiled & edited by Mary Heneghan

First Published in 2016 by
BODHICHARYA PUBLICATIONS
Bodhicharya Publications is a Community Interest Company registered in the UK.
38 Moreland Avenue, Hereford, HR1 1BN, UK
www.bodhicharya.org Email: publications@bodhicharya.org

©Bodhicharya Publications

Ringu Tulku asserts the moral right to be identified as the author of this work.
Please do not reproduce any part of this book without permission from the publisher.
We welcome the creation of editions of our books in other languages. Please contact the publisher for details.

ISBN 978-0-9576398-9-8
First Edition: March 2016

Compiled & edited by Mary Heneghan

Source: *Vajrasattva retreat* Bodhicharya Meditation Centre, Sikkim, India; November 2010. Recorded by Bernie Vorster. Transcribed and edited by Mary Heneghan.

Root text from: *Brief Recitations for the Four Preliminary Practices* by His Holiness the 17th Karmapa. © 2006 His Holiness the Gyalwang 17th Karmapa, Ogyen Drodul Trinley Dorje. English translation compiled and revised by Tyler Dewar based upon previous translations by Ari Goldfield and Karma Choephel, April 2008. Published by Nalandabodhi Publications and, previously, Tsurphu Labrang. Reproduced here with permission.

Bodhicharya Publications team for this book: Mary Heneghan; Martin Hird; Mariette van Lieshout; Rachel Moffitt; Paul O'Connor; Karma Wangmo.

Typesetting & Design by Paul O'Connor at Judo Design, Ireland.
Cover image: Huay Mae Khamin, Waterfall in Deep Forest of Thailand ©Adobe Stock
Inside colour image of Vajrasattva © R.D.Salga, Nepal: www.facebook.com/ExquisiteTibetanArt
Picture of Bell and Dorje: photography by Peter Budd.
Calligraphies of the hundred-syllable and six-syllable Vajrasattva mantras: by Tashi Mannox, Tibetan Calligraphy Artist © Tashi Mannox, see tashimannox.com.
Mantra garland designed by Paul O'Connor.

The Heart Wisdom Series

By Ringu Tulku Rinpoche

The Ngöndro
Foundation Practices of Mahamudra

From Milk to Yoghurt
A Recipe for Living and Dying

Like Dreams and Clouds
Emptiness and Interdependence, Mahamudra and Dzogchen

Dealing with Emotions
Scattering the Clouds

Journey from Head to Heart
Along a Buddhist Path

Riding Stormy Waves
Victory over the Maras

Being Pure
The practice of Vajrasattva

Radiance of the Heart
Kindness, Compassion, Bodhicitta

Meeting Challenges
Unshaken by Life's Ups and Downs

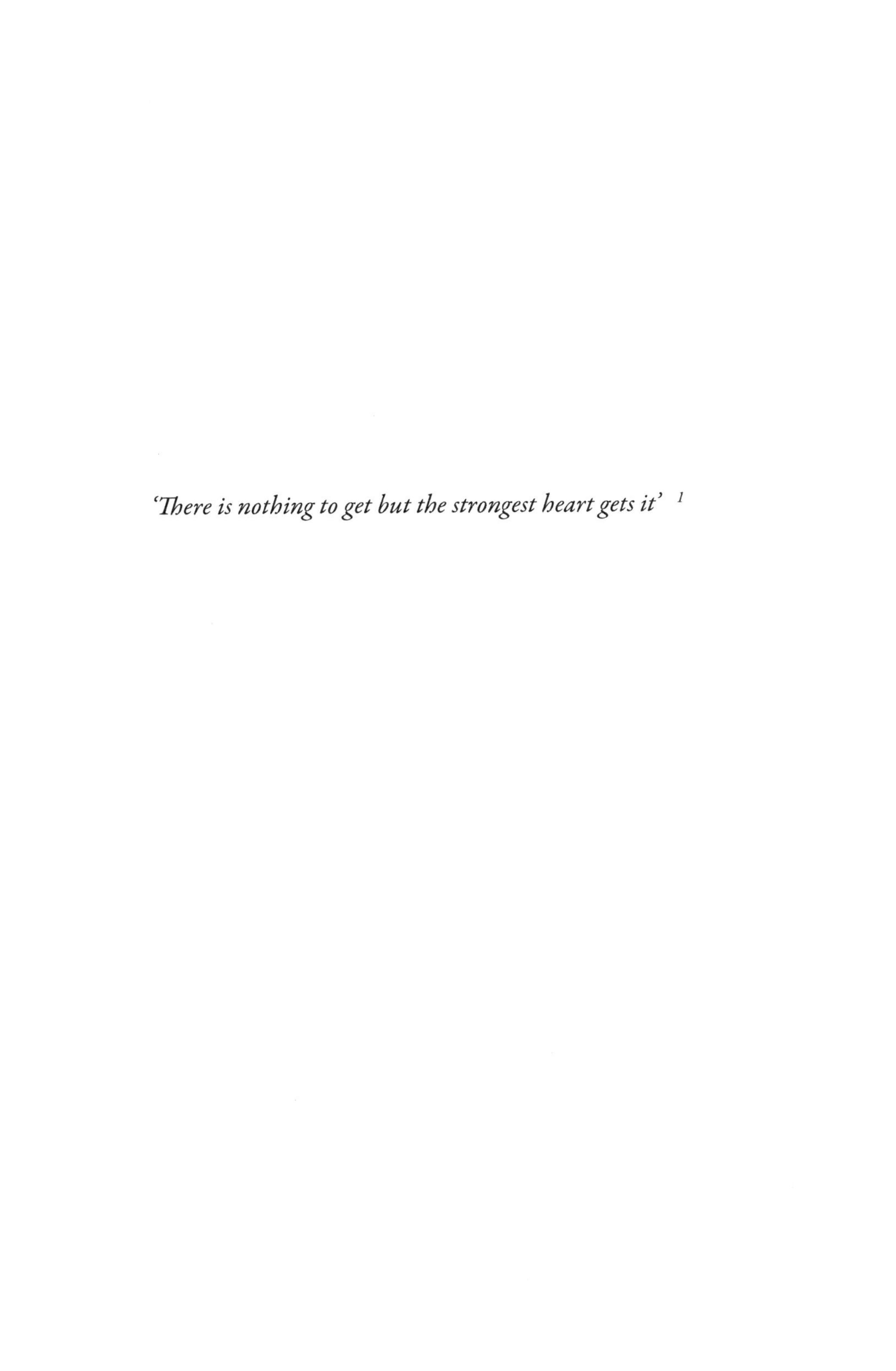

'There is nothing to get but the strongest heart gets it' [1]

Contents

Editor's Preface   xi

Introduction   1

Taking Refuge   7

The Practice of Vajrasattva   17

Setting the Practice in Context   43

Questions and Answers   65

A Short Teaching on the Bardos   79

Root Text   99

Glossary and Notes   113

Acknowledgements   127

About the Author   129

Editor's Preface

The main text of this book comes from Ringu Tulku's teachings given at a retreat for the practice of Vajrasattva, which was held at Bodhicharya Meditation Centre in Sikkim, India, in November 2010. Small additions come from the editor's own notes made at the time of that retreat and later conversations with Ringu Tulku. Another minor source of additions were notes made during a talk Ringu Tulku gave in Nottingham in May 2008, as part of a series of teachings by His Holiness the Dalai Lama, who also gave the Vajrasattva empowerment at that time.

The practice of Vajrasattva is one of the skillful means taught within the Vajrayana, the vehicle of the Buddha's teachings which traditionally takes the result as the path and which is particularly concerned therefore with 'pure view.' As Ringu Tulku might say, 'If you want to be a certain way, you have to practise being that way; you have to just *do* it.' And so the practices outlined in this book give us a way in, to do just that: to see purely, to experience *being pure*. The Vajrayana provides these kind of direct and experiential methods of practice because something powerful is needed to cut through the heavy accumulation of habits that obscure our fundamentally pure, true nature.

The potency of these methods can only achieve good results, however, when practised in the correct context. So, the Vajrayana very much includes, and is built upon the foundation, of all the general Buddhist teachings. These set the practices in context, rooting them in the wider meaning of the Buddhadharma. This is key because we have to understand how any practice works, and the wider meanings it points to, to enable it to really work on us.

Ringu Tulku goes through the practice of Vajrasattva in detail here, including the initial practice of Taking Refuge. And he also gives us much to consider in terms of the wider context we undertake these practices in: What is our motivation? What do we need to work on to tame our mind? What really *is* purification? What does it mean to be wise? Or compassionate? How can we cultivate these qualities? Ringu Tulku shows how all our understanding of Dharma can be poured into a relatively simple practice, such as the one given here. And so it becomes a deep and profound practice. As he says, 'Then, through the practice of Vajrasattva alone, you can become enlightened.'

A bonus, included in this book, is a short teaching by Ringu Tulku on the Bardos. This arose from a request by a student at the retreat and is included here because, as Ringu Tulku mentions, the Bardo teachings are connected with Vajrasattva. Rinpoche talks about the Four Bardos - of Life and Death, of Dharmata and Becoming - and shows how, at every step through the cycles of birth and death, we are given opportunities to awaken to our true nature and realise Vajrasattva, or realise ourselves as we really are.

In this way, we hope this book has something to offer for everyone: For people new to Dharma and to the Vajrayana, everything is described from a fresh start – some people on the initial retreat had never done Vajrayana practices before. This book also has plenty to offer long term practitioners, because Ringu Tulku has gone into these subtle and key topics of Dharma in a very clear way; he takes us right to their heart and brings the light of understanding there.

———

While I was working on this book, I came across a couple of instances that really made an impression on me. I'd like to share them briefly because, even though I'm sure there are layers of understanding held within them that I have not grasped yet, maybe they will spark off some understanding of your own, or curiosity. And maybe you might contemplate such things as you go forward to read Rinpoche's teachings here. My examples are both 'teachings from nature,' in a way; a quiet but universal kind of a teacher.

Firstly, I learned how diamonds are formed in nature. As you will know, the *vajra* of Vajrasattva's name, is often translated as 'diamond-like.' [Ringu Tulku gives more on the meaning of *vajra* in the text. And *sattva* means 'hero' or 'brave one.'] Apparently, diamonds are made deep beneath the earth's crust, through intense heat and pressure acting upon carbon. This process results in the form of the diamond, the hardest substance on earth, able to cut through anything and unable to be destroyed. If you want to cut a diamond, you can only use another diamond. 'So, what kind of process would parallel this in ourselves?' I wondered, since we are part of nature too. What could bring out our utterly pure, and therefore indestructible, quality?

The vajra state of mind alludes to the kind of wisdom that is indestructible; it cannot be cut down or cut through by anything else, because it sees reality as it is, completely and untainted. It passes undeterred through life, and death. I found it interesting that, in nature, diamonds are formed under intense heat and pressure. Especially as we ourselves are made up of carbon compounds, as all organic life is. Maybe everything that matures and ripens us could be likened to the heat that forms the diamonds. And isn't it true that it is often when we are under intense pressure in life that we really transform? – When we come up against ourselves in a seeming-impasse, that is when we have no choice but to transform, genuinely.

The other instance I came across was during a long sequence of pujas [or ritual chanting of prayers], I was attending in a temple some years back. As we were doing these hours and hours of puja recitation, my mind started to wander, in a spacious kind of way. I was watching the shrine activities as we recited mantras to call forth the guru and purify the water in the vase on the shrine. 'Are our mantras really purifying this water?' I thought to myself. So, I was pondering it a bit... until I realised,

'But it is water! It is this amazing, beautiful, clear, wet, flowing stuff that has miraculously arisen - we don't really know exactly how - and it sustains all of life.' This water is already pure. This water is perfectly and utterly pure. It is just as it is. How could it be otherwise?

It may be worth noticing that I saw this while inside the practice we were doing. The shrine rituals and the practices, as I understand it, work with our perception. This is the pivot of samsara and nirvana. We get stuck in a clouded, mundane way of seeing things and we forget that vast expanse of miraculous life we are part of at every moment. The practice is to shift our view so we can connect with the innate purity of life: the innate purity of water, which is also the innate purity of ourselves.

———

We would like to dedicate this book to the happy freedom of all; the quality of mind the Dharma can bring. And, in particular, I would like to dedicate my part in this work to my daughter Katie. Her name means 'pure' and she has taught me much about being in such a way. When she was a baby I used to get the funny feeling of 'missing being with her,' even though she was right there with me all day: a little bundle of purity being whisked along to shops and walks and swimming pools. Whatever the equivalents are in your own life, I think there may be something key being shown to us from such experiences.

So, through our practice, may we all learn to experience things in their complete purity. And have the courage and clarity to be purely who we really are. May all beings become free from the bondage of clouded and distorted views and dwell, instead, in the pristine awareness of Vajrasattva.

Mary Dechen Jinpa
On behalf of Bodhicharya Publications
Oxford, November 2015

Introduction

Vajrayana practice

From a general point of view, there are three vehicles of Buddhist teachings: First, Theravada Buddhism, or more correctly the Sravakayana, is based on the common and uncontroversial teachings of the Buddha. Then, Mahayana Buddhism includes all the Theravada teachings and also brings in the concept of a Bodhisattva, so the main focus is on Bodhicitta and compassion - the motivation of the Bodhisattva. The third vehicle, the Vajrayana, takes all these teachings as part of itself also. Vajrayana practice is not something separate – it needs the Theravada and Mahayana teachings as its basis and accepts all of them. So, therefore, if you are practising Vajrayana, you are practising all three vehicles.

A Vajrayana practitioner has to take core Buddhist principles, like Bodhicitta and the Six Paramitas, very much to heart. On top of that, they can also use special skilful means to transform and work on habitual tendencies. Anyone, at any level, can start on the Vajrayana path; it is not that you need to be a special kind of a person to take this path. But it can become a very swift path. It is possible that someone could even become enlightened in one lifetime. But they would need to work very hard, with a lot of commitment, and develop a lot of good qualities.

Vajrayana practice takes the result as the path. For example, if you want to be a certain way, you need to accustom yourself to being that way. Whether it is being peaceful or being joyful or whatever, you have to get used to being like that. You need to, directly, *be* like that. However, we cannot always manage it. So then, when it doesn't come so easily, one thing we can do is to take a good example to inspire us; to encourage and remind us. We absorb our mind in that example and slowly we can then become like it. The Buddha is one such example – showing us complete wisdom, complete compassion; fully enlightened.

Then we can use a form to visualise this example because, actually, we relate all our feelings to a form in one way or another. Vajrasattva was a Bodhisattva who dedicated all his energy, all his accomplishments and all his good deeds, towards the purification of all negativities. So, when he became enlightened, he became the Buddha of purification. It does not matter in this context whether such a person actually existed or not. We can use them as an example, and gain benefit and inspiration from that, regardless.

However, Buddhism is not 'atheist;' it is 'non-theistic.' While Buddhism does not teach there is one 'creator' God, we do believe in the existence of many beings of great power – Buddhas and Bodhisattvas. They may not be able to take all your negativity away from you, but they can bestow blessings and give an indication of how to practise yourself, of the way to go. This is one way we can see the practice of Vajrasattva: as an example. Before we look more specifically at this practice, we will consider two or three general practicalities.

Learning to let things be

A very important thing for practice or retreat is learning how to be relaxed. I don't mean getting up late, watching television and partying! I mean being okay with how things are. When things around you are fine, and you are okay inside, that is one thing. But when things around you are difficult, or you have difficult emotions or illness, then that is harder, but you can still be okay with that. It is about learning – deeply – to *let be*. And this is a very important attitude during practice.

When you can truly let be, it is possible to do many things and still be relaxed inside; to be relaxed in the way you do them. Of course, it is harder to remain relaxed with things when you have a lot of things to do. So, that is why we first learn how to be relaxed when we don't have anything we have to do. This is the purpose of retreat.

Doubts are natural

It is perfectly natural during the course of any practices you do, to have doubts. It is said that if you are without doubts, it is either because you are enlightened or because you have become a little bit foolish. If you are enlightened, you will know because there will be no more problems! – You will be totally happy. So, if there are still a few problems and everything is not completely fine, and you are without any doubts, you have probably become a little bit foolish! So, it is normal and okay to have doubts and they should not put you off doing practice.

Retreat structure

Generally speaking, for example in traditional three-year retreats or other Eastern, or Tibetan, types of retreat, most of the practices are done on your own, in your own room. But sometimes, especially for people who are beginning a practice, or who are not too familiar with it, then it is better to do the practice together, with others also. This Vajrasattva retreat was designed with some practice sessions done individually, alone, and some practice sessions done together as a group, each day.

The usual structure of a retreat is to have four sessions a day. You can have six sessions but it is more usual to have four:

- A dawn session, before breakfast – and usually in the East breakfast is very early so dawn sessions sometimes start at 3am or 4am. But I suggested participants should not get up too early – because I am very compassionate! So, there was a short session before breakfast.

- A morning session, after breakfast and before lunch.
- An afternoon session.
- An evening session, after dinner.

Lunch usually includes a break or some time off in the middle part of the day. Then, you can make the sessions longer or shorter. In this retreat, we made the first and last sessions short and the others longer - two hours - which is okay, but is quite short by usual standards. But, in one way, the sessions are not the most important thing.

The whole time you are in retreat, whether you are 'in session' or 'outside session,' is the retreat. Sometimes 'out of session' is more important than 'in session.' During sessions you only do the practice that you are supposed to be doing. Usually, people don't read books or do anything else, during sessions, other than the specific practice.

When you are between sessions, then you can read books or teachings or do other Dharma-related activities; that is the general way. At that time, you choose what you want to do – you can take a walk, you can take a nap, you can discuss with other people. It is important to realise you don't need to fight with yourself; you can choose what you want to do between sessions. This is to give some outline of the general structure of a retreat. Now, we will turn to the actual practice.

Overview of the practice of Vajrasattva

We are looking at the practice of Vajrasattva, but 'Vajrasattva' is not just one practice. It is a whole collection of practices. There are many different types of Vajrasattva practice. Some are many hundreds of pages long. Some can be just three pages long, or one page, or even half a page. The practice can become very elaborate. Some versions include one hundred peaceful and wrathful deities; others include the Five Buddha Families. Some are much simpler and have Vajrasattva visualised alone.

There are many lineages of Vajrasattva practice: some come from way, way back and some are more contemporary, found through *termas* [treasure findings], usually associated with Guru Rinpoche. It is said that Guru Pema [Guru Padmasambhava / Guru Rinpoche] hid many *termas* in Tibet to be found by later disciples or emanations of him.

Through Vajrasattva, you can do all sorts of practices. When we say 'Vajrasattva practice,' it does not mean just praying to one Buddha or making a connection with one enlightened being. That is not the point. Vajrasattva practice is a whole set of practices. For example, you can do yoga through Vajrasattva practice. You can do *Tummo* or *Tsa Lung* or *Pranayama* practice through Vajrasattva. You can also do *Phowa* through Vajrasattva practice. You can do all sorts of different things. We are not looking at these here - partly because we don't have too much time, but also because I myself don't like things to be too complicated.

I like to keep things simple and, in fact, I am not good at complicated things. So, I assume it is the same for you. Or, even if you are good at complicated things, there is no point spending a lot of time learning complicated things and then never having the time to practise them. So, we choose the simplest form of Vajrasattva practice to do, and then we try to include *in that* all the wider teachings and understandings behind it. This is what we will try to do here.

We already looked at the basic approach of any Vajrayana practice, of which Vajrasattva is an example. And we mentioned how important it is to appreciate Vajrayana practice is not separate from the general Buddhist practices. It is held within the general Buddhist practices and has to be practised in that way. So, it starts with turning your mind towards reflecting on how you see your life and the world; how you see things generally. It has to start from here. This is why we start with refuge.

Taking Refuge

Buddha, Dharma and Sangha

Refuge is about laying a foundation for your practice. It is about finding a direction you want to go in. I usually describe it as finding a purpose and a path for yourself. In Buddhism, we go for refuge to the Buddha, Dharma and Sangha. Going for refuge to the Buddha is not about asking Buddha to come and help you, and save you. That is not going for refuge. That is prayer, and you can do that also, that is okay from the Buddhist point of view. But refuge is something a little bit different.

Refuge is based on an understanding that there is a possibility of transformation. The Buddha is the ideal, or example, of transformation. When we describe Buddha, we say that anybody who has limitless wisdom and compassion, is a Buddha. But it is important to understand that 'Buddha' or 'enlightenment' is not a result of attaining something that you do not have, now. It is more the result of getting rid of something. Like, for instance, if you are locked in a room and then you get out of that room. It is a result, but you have not got anything you did not have before. You got out of something that you were caught in.

In a similar way, Buddhahood is seen as freeing yourself from ignorance. You could also say, it is freeing yourself from something a bit like an addiction. If you have been addicted to something, or under the influence of a very negative habitual tendency, and then you break out of it, reaching Buddhahood would be like that. It is about *breaking out* of our usual, limited way of being.

So, when we say 'going for refuge to Buddha,' we are saying: 'I, and every being, has that capacity to be free from suffering, from ignorance, from negative ways of reacting; and from these very strong negative emotions and reactions which create a lot of pain and problems for myself and others. There is a possibility to change this, and I would like to work on this, to free myself from my habitual tendencies, my ignorance and my negative emotions.'

So going for refuge to the Buddha is deciding that I want to transform and I also want to help others to transform. Transform means 'become better,' not just a little bit, but completely. The Buddha is the utmost kind of transformation. So when I say I go for refuge to the Buddha, what I mean is that I would like to transform completely: I want to develop my compassion, my wisdom and my ability to help others, to the utmost. This means understanding that there is the seed, or the potential, of compassion in me, and the seed, or potential, of wisdom in me. This is what we sometimes call Buddhanature.

When we talk about Buddhanature, it doesn't mean to say we are all really good; we are all good, there is no real problem, we are already Buddha. That is not what it means. What it means to say is that we are not all good; we have lots of negativity; we have lots of delusions, lots of negative emotions and lots of negative habitual tendencies. We are not much better than animals. Our 'animal instinct' is still very much there. But we have progressed a little bit; we have evolved a little bit. And we can evolve much more. That is the idea, that there is a possibility to do that. That is why we say we have Buddhanature. We have some wisdom, some compassion, some little bit of loving-kindness and all these can be developed and increased.

So, going for refuge to the Buddha means that I want to free myself from the causes and conditions that make me chained to the problems and suffering of ignorance. And I would like to find ways and means to work on that, not only for myself, but for others also. So, once I have gone for refuge to the Buddha, then I have to find a way of how to do that.

This is going for refuge to the Dharma. The Dharma is the methods: the teachings of the Buddha and the experience of those teachings. When I say I take refuge in Dharma, again, it is not like saying, 'Please Dharma, come and save me!' Because there is nothing called 'Dharma' that can do that. Dharma consists of all the methods to work on myself; all the different ways, means, understandings and practices, whatever needs to be done. These methods are the Dharma and I need to learn these.

So, going for refuge to the Dharma is saying I would like to try and learn them and then I would like to use them, apply them and practise them; so that I use them on myself and my experience. So, Dharma is described as both aspects: the teaching and the experience. The teaching is the learning and the experience is that understanding becoming part of ourselves. When it has become our experience, we actually act in that way. It becomes part of who we are.

Then there is going for refuge to the Sangha. The Sangha is the people who have experience of the Dharma. So Sangha can be very high, like Buddha Shakyamuni. Buddha Shakyamuni is also Sangha. When Buddha Shakyamuni became enlightened, it is said that there was one Sangha in the world. So it is not necessary for it to be a group of people, although the word 'sangha' means an assembly or a group of people or an association. But it doesn't mean that in a Buddhist sense. And then when Buddha taught the first of his teachings to five of his first disciples and they became enlightened, they became Arhats; then it is said that there were six Sangha members.

So the actual, true Sangha is anybody who has true experience of Dharma. This is not just the learning of Dharma but also the actualisation of the experience of Dharma; those who have actually transformed at some level. That is the real Sangha, the true Sangha. Those who are not truly experienced but have some understanding and are trying to work on that, a group of people who are working on that, can also be called a Sangha. They are trying to understand the Dharma and practise it. That can also be called a Sangha, an ordinary Sangha. Sometimes they call it a Beginner's Sangha.

When I say I go for refuge to the Sangha, it means 'How do I learn the Dharma?' I want to learn; I am ready to learn from people who have some understanding or experience. That means I want to open myself to study and learn and receive instructions and examples and methods. Also, I open myself to be positively influenced. Learning is not only in theory. Learning is through inspiration and influence also.

Sometimes we talk about transmission. Especially in Vajrayana Buddhism, we talk about transmission. What is transmission? It is nothing like: the teacher comes and makes a symbolic action or something and something comes out of the teacher and goes into you. Transmission is that you come into contact with a genuine Master, a genuine Dharma person, or not even necessarily Dharma, but a great person. And then, through his or her being, through their teaching and way of being – in body, speech and mind – you are influenced; you kind of change, either knowingly or unknowingly. So, you change for the better. That is transmission.

This is our natural way of learning and is how we learn from everything. It is how we learn from our society; how we learn from our parents and how we learn from our peers and our teachers. It is not just what they say. We learn by looking at what they do and how they are. That is the same thing; that is transmission.

So, therefore, going for refuge to the Sangha is saying that I would like to make myself open, with humility, in order to learn. That is one way of going for refuge to the Sangha. I allow myself to be influenced positively. And I do not allow myself to be influenced negatively. This humility is very important. It is said that if you have pride you cannot learn anything. You are closed, as if you think: 'I know everything, I don't need anything. I look at everybody like they are useless.' Then you cannot learn anything from anybody. The more I see the positive qualities in others, the more I myself can learn. If I can see even little positive qualities in others, some good side of them, some small good quality; the more I see this, the more I learn, the more I acquire good qualities and the more I improve.

If you don't see any positive qualities in anybody, it doesn't mean that you are the best. It means that you are closed. You cannot learn anything while you are like that and you will remain like that always if you keep that attitude. That is what we are saying when we talk about humility and humbleness: not to be coated with pride, but to allow ourselves to soak up positive qualities and positive things from outside, from everybody and everything.

It is not that I have to only see good things and I cannot see bad things. That is not the idea. Of course, we have to understand the bad sides also. We don't need to close our eyes to them. We have to be very aware and alert and understand and be clear, but not be clear *only* about bad things. We have to be clear and understand and be aware of the positive things *as much as* the other side. So the more we can be aware of the positive things, the more we can also feel good about that. We can learn and we can respect others. Respect is a very important thing because it is the beginning of learning. It is the beginning of our improvement also. And it is the beginning of the Sangha, of togetherness - respect for each other and showing appreciation for each other. That is what leads to togetherness and Sangha.

The story of the three priests

There is a story of three priests who had a small Catholic church. They were alone and rather old and no new people were coming to their monastery or their church. These three priests were very much trying to get the monastery and the church to prosper and grow and to bring lots of people there. But they were not succeeding. Then one day they heard that a wise man had come into the locality and they wanted to go and ask him for some advice on how to change this. So they sent one of the priests to see him and ask for his advice. He went to the man and asked, 'We have this little church but we are only three people and nobody else is coming. There are no new monks in the monastery. It is all kind of dying out. We tried all sorts of things but they have not worked. What can we do? Can you give us some advice?'

The wise man said, 'It is what this time now is like – people have become so materialistic. They are not interested in religion. I don't know what to do because it is just like this; it is the time.' He didn't have any special advice. So the priest said, 'Thank you very much' and went to go. But then just as he was leaving, the wise man said, 'By the way, one of you three is the Messiah.'

So, the priest went back to the other two who were waiting for him to come back. They asked him, 'What did he say, what did he say?' 'Well,' he said, 'Nothing special. It is the time he said, everybody has become too materialistic. He didn't have any particular advice. But he said something very strange at the end.' 'What did he say?' the others asked. 'He said that one of us three is the Messiah.' So they laughed and said that it must have been a joke.

In the evening they went to bed, and then they started to think. One of them was thinking, 'Maybe it is possible that one of the Fathers *is* the one? Maybe Father Peter is, maybe he is the one? Maybe he is the Messiah, because he is so good? He is very good and very learned and knows lots of things. He *could* be the Messiah.' And then Father Peter was thinking, 'Maybe Father John is the one. He could be – he is so kind and so compassionate and so nice to people. He could be the one.' And Father John was thinking, 'It is possible Father Patrick is the one. He is so good, so simple and so humble. Maybe he is the one?'

Then the next morning when they came out and saw each other again, they were so nice to each other, they were so respectful to each other. Because the other one could be the Messiah. Then somebody came to visit and he was so impressed because he thought they were so nice and so kind to each other here. Everyone was respectful to each other so he liked very much the atmosphere. Then another person came and it was the same way. More and more people came and in a few years the church started to revive and became very active and prosperous. So it worked!

This is what Sangha is – to respect each other. But respect is not like: 'I *must* respect him. I don't want to respect him but I must.' That doesn't work. You look for some good qualities, some good things of this person, because everybody has good sides, and then you can appreciate them. It doesn't mean we can't see anything else there. Of course there are bad things there too. We need to accept that that is there. All of us have some good qualities and some not so good things.

Why a refuge ceremony?

Once I have decided that this is the path I am going to follow and this is how I want to work on myself, it is possible to take refuge in front of a Lama, as a ceremony. This does not mean that I take on any kind of a dogma or set of beliefs or anything like that. Usually we say if you take refuge then you can call yourself a Buddhist, but it is not like you are joining a group or a club. It is nothing like that. There is nothing to 'leave' to become a Buddhist. It is about deciding the direction you would like to follow, the way you would like to go, how you would like to move forward in your life. Once you have reached that point, then you have actually taken refuge, because that decision is the refuge.

You do not take refuge *from* a lama, you take refuge *in front of* a lama. The lama is just witnessing it in a way. You are not taking refuge *in* the lama. It is a little bit like when you want to make a decision and you need to finalise it, you have to have some kind of a reference point to make it more concrete because you will need to remind yourself of it again and again.

Our mind is very flexible, too flexible sometimes. If I meet with a positive kind of an influence today then I go in a positive way today, but tomorrow it may be different. If I go with drinkers, I can become a drinker. If I go with people who meditate, I can become someone who meditates. When I take this refuge and decide this is what I want to work on, it is easy to remember now, but even in a few days time I may find it not as easy. It is when you find yourself doing something that is not-so-right, that is the time that you need to remind yourself and say to yourself, 'No, this is not the right way. I have taken refuge. I decided I wanted to go in *this* way. And I did not do it just because somebody told me to do it or something like that. I have thought about it and I made a decision. I decided that it was good for me and good for others.'

When you take refuge in front of a Lama in this way, you get a new name, also for this reason. It is a reminder. What is written in the name is not so important. People think maybe you are given a name of something you need to work on. They think the lama has 'chosen' you, in a way, to work on that. It is not like that, for me anyway. You can work on it if you like, there is no problem with that approach. But mainly the name is there as a reminder of taking refuge.

The actual ceremony is very simple. Usually we make three prostrations and that is there because the Buddha himself actually instructed his monks and his followers *not* to teach or give any instructions or any ordinations without being asked - and asked at least three times. So the three prostrations are to ask three times. Then we say the refuge prayer, asking to take refuge until we attain enlightenment and to be seen as having taken refuge from this moment on. That is the Mahayana way.

Then I cut a piece of the person's hair and this is to represent that they are making the highest offering to the Buddha, Dharma and Sangha. Hair is a part of yourself, a part of your body, and it is also growing on the highest part of yourself, so giving a little bit of that as an offering represents that the person is making the highest offering. Then the person is given a new name to represent that they have started a new way of life. Then they are given a blessing cord, which is just the Tibetan style, and then we make a dedication. That is the ceremony for taking refuge.

The Practice of Vajrasattva

The practice we are going to use here comes from the text 'Brief Recitations for the Four Preliminary Practices.' This text covers the Four Extraordinary Practices of the *Ngöndro*, and this version was composed in 2006, especially for Western practitioners, by His Holiness the 17th Karmapa. His instructions were that if a Tibetan wants to practise these, they have to get special permission; but everybody else can practise them once they have had the *lung* (the reading transmission) and other empowerments.

The practices given here do not have as many words as more traditional versions, which is why I have chosen this text to use as the Vajrasattva practice here. Each practice session you can do the Refuge practice and then the Vajrasattva practice and then do dedications at the end.

Refuge

We have already looked at the meaning of taking refuge. When we go for refuge to the Buddha, Dharma and Sangha, then we are practising Dharma. We are actually having a path and we are actually training ourselves on it. Therefore, going for refuge is actually very important and is the basis of the path. It is about our whole way of life. So, taking refuge is not something that we do once and then it is done and finished. It is a practice. It is a way of life and something we remind ourselves of, again and again. At the start of every day and at the beginning of every practice session we remind ourselves that this is the way we have chosen to go in, and how we need to work on it.

The Vajrayana elaborates on the principle of refuge we have discussed so far, and there are further refuges as well as the three of Buddha, Dharma and Sangha. The practice we are doing here gives five refuges altogether. Generally, in Vajrayana practice we also go for refuge to the Lamas, the Yidams and the Khandros (Tibetan) or Dakinis (Sanskrit). Here the Yidams and Khandros, or Dakinis, are included together as one refuge.

The Lama is like the Buddha – someone who has experience of the Dharma, who holds the lineage or experience, so that is similar to the Buddha. That is the principle of the Lama in the Vajrayana. The Yidam is the practice or the teaching, so it is like the Dharma. Vajrasattva is an example of a Yidam. That is the practice. It is not different from the Dharma, it is the same. And then the Khandros or Dakinis are the people who are practising the Vajrayana practice. So, therefore, they are the Sangha. In this particular text we recite it in this way:

'All sentient beings and I go for refuge to the Gurus.

We go for refuge to the Yidams.

We go for refuge to the Buddhas.

We go for refuge to the Dharma.

We go for refuge to the Sangha.'

The text says,

'Go to these five jewels for refuge as many times as possible.'

Now, why does it say 'All sentient beings and I'? This is because we are using this recitation as a practical meditation, as an exercise. So, we use a certain kind of visualisation with the recitation, to make it more of a practical exercise, and this is part of that. Many Western people say that 'visualising' is very difficult to do, that it sounds complicated or unusual.

But actually it is very simple, and something everybody does all the time. Generally speaking, we can think of, or remember, a place far away or somewhere that is not here right now. We could see that in our mind's eye, how it looks. We could think about something nice or not so nice, and we can see that vividly in our mind. That is visualising something.

So we can use visualising something, like a specific time or a place or a person, to associate with feeling nice and wonderful and positive. And, through that, we can feel warm and contented and relaxed, or even blissful. Similarly, we could think about times in our life that have not gone so well or were difficult or hard and then we may not feel so good. This can even affect how our body works - our heart rate and blood pressure change by changing how we are thinking. So, what I think about, and what I focus on, is very important. Actually, what I become is due to what I think, how I feel and how I experience. So, if I am more used to dwelling on the positive side of things, seeing the positive side of myself and others, then I become a happier and more positive person. I may even become a more successful person. But if I only concentrate on negative or problematic things, I become more tense and strained and unhappy.

So, what we will become is very much in our hands. All these practices are about how to train ourselves to become more positive, that is the practice. So we use this method of visualising in many different ways. And here we use it also in the refuge.

We start by visualising a very big lake: nice and calm, filled with cool, pure, fresh water. You can have fishes and birds in your visualisation, and things like that. But the main thing is, it is a very open and very spacious feeling. That is important, because how I actually feel is very much dependent on where I am and how I see things. If we are in a very pleasant, calm and quiet place, usually we naturally feel good. Being in nature is nice for us because nature is like that: It brings us contentment and peace to feel in contact with nature, with the natural ground. So this is why we use something pleasant like this as our visualisation.

The spaciousness is very important, also. We need to train our mind to be spacious. This is not just a preliminary, but is also the main practice. Because how much problem we have, is totally dependent on how spacious our mind is. When my mind feels 'small' or constrained, I get upset very easily - my mind reacts to little things in a big way; I simply cannot bear things to go wrong in even very small ways. I have very fixed ideas and can only be content if things happen according to how I think they should. But, the more spacious my mind is, the less I become tense or taken over by negative emotions and reactions.

In everything, the more space I have in my mind, the more peaceful I become. This is very, very important. It is like, for example, how the sky is very, very big so it doesn't matter if there are a few clouds in it. The clouds don't disturb it. So therefore, we need to learn to think with a lot of space - to *feel* with a lot of space. It doesn't matter how big or small your room is. You can have a very small room with a very small bed but if your mind is spacious, it is okay. Whereas, even if you have a big room and a big space to be in, but your mind is tight, then it feels constrained and crowded. So, we bring in this feeling of spaciousness.

Then, in the centre of that lake, you see a beautiful tree. The more beautiful and artistic you can make it, the better, because beauty also brings peace to your mind. Beauty makes your mind feel beautiful, comfortable and feeling good. When you see something beautiful, you become joyful, happy and content. So we visualise a beautiful tree. Sometimes they talk about it being made of precious stones or something like that but the important thing is it is very beautiful.

In the centre of the tree you see the Lama, who is your root guru if you have one, with all the lineage around him. Or you can see Vajrasattva in the centre in this case, as we are practising Vajrasattva. You can see the form of Vajrasattva as representing the essence of all the enlightened gurus. And then all the enlightened beings, who have experience of the Dharma, who your teaching comes from, all of them are there too. You don't have to recognise them all individually, you can just feel they are there.

The Dharma, in the form of books and texts, and the Sangha, including all the Arhats and Bodhisattvas, and the Yidams are all there, arranged as the text says. Everybody is there; everybody who has crossed the samsaric state of mind, who has the wisdom and compassion and the power to transform and help other beings. This includes all compassionate beings, not just Buddhists. You feel that it is like a mandala, or field, of every enlightened being there. They are all full of compassion, as if seeing each being as their only child and wanting to help them. And they have the capacity and wisdom to help. As much as possible, you imagine or feel they are like that.

There is an important point to be made here. Generally in life, if I have received plenty of love, then I can love. How do I learn to love? – by feeling loved, by feeling people taking care of me. Feeling that shows me how to love and that is how I learn. So, here I feel all these enlightened beings to be radiating unconditional love, limitless kindness and compassion. Usually, our only examples of love are our parents and friends and partners etc. But they are human beings and sometimes, when they are not perfect, we get disappointed and feel nobody can love properly. But that is not true. They are human beings, like ourselves, and have their own problems. We are all still in samsara. So, if we want to learn this kind of limitless love and compassion, we have to find someone else, not just our parents and our friends, to give us this example. So this is why we feel the presence of all these enlightened beings.

This is practising feeling wisdom and compassion, because, the more I feel the presence of these beings radiating this feeling, the more I am feeling it myself. Who is feeling all this? None other than myself. I am feeling it. I am generating that feeling. My mind is feeling it. So, when I am feeling the presence of Buddhas who are completely compassionate and wise and giving blessing, then I am actually exercising that feeling.

Not in a theoretical way, but in a practical way, because my mind is actually feeling that. Therefore, it is actually working on me; I am training myself using that method.

Then, at the same time, I feel that I am present together with all the other sentient beings like myself, alongside me: my parents, my relatives, my friends and also my enemies. I feel all the human beings to be present, and then also all the other beings, like the animals. I feel the presence of all the beings together with me - because who do I want to help, if not them? They all want to be free from suffering; they all want to be happy, with a totally lasting happiness and joy. I feel all of them sitting here with me in the same group.

When I do this, I am naturally generating compassion towards them, because I am including them. Everybody is there equally, people I know and people I don't know; there are no 'strangers.' When I feel that, I am also extending my mind. I am not only focussing on myself and my nearest and dearest, I am including everyone. My family is not only my wife and children; my family is all of these people. When I try and see things this way, I am making my mind more spacious and also I am generating compassion towards them because I am putting everyone together, equally important.

When I recite my prayer, I feel that some kind of blessings, or light, that can bring transformation, comes from the refuge tree. I feel that I am receiving this light, these blessings and the power of transformation. And, not only I, but all sentient beings are receiving these. I become purified and healed and transformed. And so does every being, also.

All the negative things that I have accumulated are gone. All the resulting negative things – like pain and tension and disease - have gone. But, also, so have the causes of them – all the negative emotions and habitual tendencies. These are all gone from myself and from all the beings. Everybody feels lighter; they feel happier; they feel well. Imagine that everybody feels like that. When I experience that everybody is feeling better, who is feeling that? It is me that is feeling that. So, naturally, I am feeling better. This is the practice of refuge. The main benefit of this practice is for myself, when I do it. But then sometimes it can also benefit others, because you are generating this for others.

When you do this practice, you can take your time over it. You can recite the refuge, again and again, if you want. Or you can just recite it once and then take time on feeling it all. This is very important to understand, because all practices are similar in this way. The essence of all the practices is the same and it is not about thinking; it is not just using seeing and thinking; it is more about *feeling*. Because what we need to transform is the way we experience things, the way we feel, and not only the way we think. Thinking is only concepts, but feeling is experience. We need to transform our experience, not only our concepts, so the main thing about the practice, is the feeling.

The recitation that goes with this visualisation comes before the refuge to the five jewels, and is said as follows:

'Before me in the sky is the Guru Vajradhara,

Surrounded by the Gurus of the lineage of meaning and blessings

And Gurus with whom I have dharmic connections of faith.

In front are the Yidams; to the right are the Buddhas.

Behind is the sacred Dharma; to the left, the Sangha.

All are surrounded by ocean-like retinues of their own kind.

My mothers, sentient beings, and I stand together

As the sources of refuge gaze down upon us.

One-pointedly, we go for refuge and arouse Bodhicitta.'

Next in the practice, we generate Bodhicitta.

Bodhicitta

The word *Bodhicitta* is a Sanskrit word. *Bodhi* means 'enlightened' and *citta* means 'heart' so it literally means 'enlightened heart.' What it is in practice is actually compassion, and usually we say 'compassion with wisdom.' So Bodhicitta is the heart of the whole Buddhist practice, especially the Mahayana path. Usually they say that the main thing in Mahayana Buddhist practice is Bodhicitta, and actually there is nothing more, other than Bodhicitta.

That is why the great Tibetan master, Patrul Rinpoche, said that everything in Dharma practice actually relates to Bodhicitta. He was one of the most learned Lamas of Tibet, ever. And he said, 'In Buddhism I have not found anything more than Bodhicitta. The essence of Buddhism is Bodhicitta. All other teachings are either a preliminary to Bodhicitta; or something that is helping to generate Bodhicitta itself; or something that is a branch or result of Bodhicitta. There is nothing else. So, therefore, everything is Bodhicitta.'

So, Bodhicitta is very important. The practice of Bodhicitta is not only a Buddhist thing. And in Buddhism we should not just adopt practices without thinking about them: 'This is the Buddhist line so, therefore, I must do this or believe this.' We need to first think, 'What is it that I really want? What is it that the truth is? What is the most important thing to me?' And then it slowly leads to this understanding. We need to look into our heart and ask, 'What is it *really* that I want? What is it that I wish most?'

What would a small child say if you asked them, in the playground, 'What is it that you really want?' They might say, 'I want to be a doctor' or 'I want to be a scientist.' Usually they say that and this is the way our society thinks. Our society is very much focussed on our profession, our means of livelihood. There is sometimes confusion between the means of a livelihood and a *life*. How I earn my living, what I *do*, becomes very important. And that becomes the focus of my life. But my life is not what I do. My life is how I live my life, and how I experience it. The means of living is a little bit different, but we sometimes mix these together.

When I really look *deeply*, and ask what it is that I want, mostly we will find, I think, that we want to be free from suffering and totally free from any negative things, and be really joyful and happy. You may want to call it something different. Every word has many different meanings. The word 'happiness' can be interpreted in many different ways, so just that word cannot say the whole thing I am meaning here. But what I really wish is something really good for myself, and freedom from suffering. And I wish that to be truly lasting, not only for a short time. And that is true for everybody. We all want to be free from every negative thing; which is what we call 'suffering' in Buddhism.

Sometimes people misunderstand this and I have heard people describing Buddhists as thinking life is only suffering. I have heard this said. It is not that Buddhists think that life is only suffering. The Buddhist understanding is that everybody wants to be *free from suffering*. It is two different things. We all know there is a lot of suffering but the view is that it is something we can be, and should be, free from. Everybody, whether you are a good person or a bad person, wants this. Even people who are doing very negative things; they may be acting unwisely, but they are doing it because they want to be happy. They are trying to become free. Even committing suicide is trying to do that: they want to be free from suffering and problems. They think that if they die then it will all be finished, although it may not happen like that. But everyone's motivation is to be free from suffering. I have been thinking about this. For example, many psychologists say that some people have a 'death wish,' but I don't think it is a death wish; I think it is the wish to be free, free from suffering.

Everybody wants to be free from pain and suffering and problems, and have lasting peace and happiness, however you describe that. When

I see that this is what I want and what everybody wants, then the most important thing becomes trying to find a way to create that situation, for myself and for others. This is what I need to dedicate my life to, and I need to dedicate all my life to it. It may be difficult; it may take a long time and so on, but this is what I would like to work on. If someone really genuinely says this, then they have Bodhicitta.

The first, real Bodhicitta is that you want to commit yourself to work towards the well being of all the beings, including yourself. You commit to work on it, step by step, and that becomes the focus. In order to do that, you may have to do different things: you may have to do this or that; you may need to rest, also; you may need to not do anything yet but just study and work on your own understanding.

So there are two things here. One is that, the more you understand that there is a possibility of doing this, the more strong and realistic you become about it. This is the wisdom, a kind of understanding that there might be a way to change myself, to transform myself. If I work on my habitual tendencies and on my negative ways of reacting, then there is a possibility of finding more peace and joy and things like that. If I don't react with so much fear, aversion, clinging and attachment, then I can face my life in a more real way. The more I understand this, the clearer I become about it and the more convinced I become. My conviction, and my experience, becomes stronger. So, therefore, the wisdom and the compassion come together.

When I feel the presence of, or know of the possibility of, enlightened beings, and then I want to work on this path; then I am generating Bodhicitta. The more I renew this understanding or this choice of direction or way of understanding, the more clear and directed I am. This is why they say that, when you generate Bodhicitta, you are on the way to Buddhahood. This is how it becomes very important. It is also compassion - practical compassion. It is not all soppy – nice, nice, only – it is about really wanting to work on that direction and do something beneficial.

So we connect with this wish and generate the mind of Bodhicitta, with the same visualisation still in place, by reciting:

'Until I reach enlightenment's essence,
I go for refuge to the Buddhas.
To the Dharma and the assembly
Of Bodhisattvas, too, I go for refuge.
Just as the Sugatas of the past
Aroused the mind of Bodhicitta;
Just as they followed step-by-step
The training of the Bodhisattvas,
So, too, shall I to benefit wanderers
Arouse the mind of Bodhicitta.
So, too, shall I follow step-by-step
The Bodhisattva's training.'

'Wanderers' here refers to all the beings (wandering) in samsara. This is Bodhicitta and these are the vows of the Bodhisattva. Even the aspiration to generate this is a very positive and a very compassionate practice, in itself. It is also a very open-minded and spacious-minded practice, because you are making a decision to work for all the beings. So you could not be more open-minded than that. They say that Bodhicitta has these four limitlessnesses, or four limitless aspects:

- It is for all the sufferings, wanting to get rid of all the sufferings: small problems, big problems, everybody's problems. There is no limit.
- It is for all the beings. I want to get rid of all the sufferings for all the beings, not just for one person, or one nation or even one kind of being, like all the human beings. This is the second limitlessness.
- It is for the highest, best-possible happiness and well-being. I don't want to just get rid of all the suffering; I want to get the highest and

best possible kind of happiness and well-being.

- It is for all time, not just a short time. I don't want people just to have a nice time for a short time, like going on a picnic; it is for all time.

These are the four limitlessnesses.

Then there is a four-line prayer, which says:

> 'May precious and supreme Bodhicitta
>
> Arise where it has not arisen,
>
> Not diminish where it has arisen,
>
> And continually increase and increase.'

It means, may every being have this attitude of Bodhicitta and, if anyone has it, may it not decrease but may it increase and increase. Because if everybody has Bodhicitta, there cannot be any problems in the world. So the easiest way of getting rid of all the problems, is for everybody to have Bodhicitta. This is not easy to achieve, of course, but if everybody really wished to help all beings, and were genuinely committed to that, then there would be no more problem among people.

> *'Finally, the sources of refuge melt into light and then become one with me.'*

> *'Second, between sessions, do not be indifferent. Take up the antidotes: Strive to increase devotion to the guru, to develop as much faith in the rare and supreme jewels as possible, and to have greater and greater compassion for sentient beings.'*

So, this is the practice of Refuge and Bodhicitta. These are the two things we start with, which are part of practice generally. How much time you want to spend on this part of the practice does not matter too much. You can spend quite a lot of time on it during your own practice, as it is important.

Vajrasattva

Generally, one should receive the empowerment of Vajrasattva in order to do the practice. The empowerment, reading transmission and explanation of a practice, together equip one to follow a certain practice. An empowerment is a blessing and is also called a transmission – a transmission of the lineage. It also serves as a teaching. So, it is all three: a blessing, a transmission and a teaching. It is a little bit like a guided meditation, something that we do together, invoking the blessings of the lineage. Once you have received the empowerment, you can follow the practice.

The practice is to recite from the text, as follows:

> 'Above the crown of my head, on a lotus-moon seat,
> Is Guru Vajrasattva, white in colour, adorned with ornaments,
> With one face and two arms,
> Holding a vajra with his right hand and a bell with his left, and
> seated in vajra posture.'

Vajrasattva is not necessarily a person but the practice is sometimes also associated with a person. There was at some time a being, whose name I don't know, who generated Bodhicitta, saying he wanted to liberate all sentient beings from suffering and bring them to lasting peace and happiness and enlightenment, and towards that he would like to work. He dedicated his life towards this and then he said he would especially like to help purify people. So, then he worked in this way for life after life after life. And he made a promise that anybody who made any connection with him in any way, with his name, would have a special power of purification. So that is why the Vajrasattva practice is supposed to be especially good for purification. But we need to truly understand the idea of purification.

Purification

The first thing is to understand: We are not what we do. If I do something wrong, that is not the only thing about who I am now. For example, if a child spills some milk, and you say, 'You are a bad child. You spilled some milk!' Then the child thinks, 'I am a bad child, because I spilled some milk.' The child is identifying him or herself with the action: 'I am the milk-spiller!' If that is really the case, then it could never be purified. Because they have become that. They have identified with that. They became the milk-spiller, and then 'the bad one.'

Maybe you spilled milk once, or twice even. But you do not need to be 'the milk-spiller.' What if someone came and said to the child, 'You did a bad thing. You spilled milk.' It can still be changed. Then the child thinks, 'Ah, I spilled milk. That was bad. But I am not the bad one. I am not the milk-spiller.'

Purification is based on that: I am not 'the bad one.' I do bad things and have done bad things, but I am not *the bad one*. Everybody does good things and bad things, everybody makes mistakes but they can also do good things. This understanding is very important. Maybe I have done bad things, and gone through bad things. Maybe I have had negative emotions and done negative actions but that goes for everybody.

Negative things can become positive things, also. I do some negative things and some positive things. I can become more positive. This is where purification lies. If I say that I am the bad one, then there is no purification possible. If I say negative things have happened, that doesn't mean that is who I am. Then purification can happen.

Therefore, you can allow the negative thing to go. You can develop your positive qualities. You can enhance your positive habitual tendencies so that you become better and better. What we are trying to do here, in the practice, is to allow those negative things that I cling to, to allow them to go. We have lots of remembered and not-remembered things we cling to; things we understand and things we don't understand, conceptual and non-conceptual, many things. We can, and we should, let them go. That is the practice.

But it is not enough just to say, 'Oh, I should let it go.' Just by saying that, it doesn't go. I have to really *let it go*, and repeatedly. It is not easy because I have so much that I hold onto. I hold on to all these negative things and negative ways of doing things. It is like a habit, an addiction. Something that has become habitual is not easy to change. So, the practice is to cultivate another habit because that is how to change the habit you already have.

So, therefore, that is the practice: learning how to feel pure; how to feel when you are not holding on to negative things; how to feel more pure and positive and compassionate. You learn how to feel like Vajrasattva, like a Buddha. You can only do that by *doing*. You cannot learn it by just having the understanding. It is like learning to drive a car. You cannot learn to drive a car by just reading the text about how to drive a car, and memorising that. You have to go and *do* it, again and again and again.

So, in the same way, we learn to be like Vajrasattva. We learn by doing it, by experiencing. We can recite the mantra and visualise Vajrasattva. Or we can do it in our daily life. Both ways are learning through experience and we have to do both these ways. That is Vajrasattva practice. Whether you want to visualise in exactly the way described or not, that is not the most important thing.

Purification actually comes about through wisdom and compassion. What purifies us is our understanding of wisdom and compassion. The strongest purification is wisdom, because it gets rid of ignorance directly. If you really reach a place of true wisdom, that is it! – All negativity will be gone. But it is not so easy to reach such a place. So, the next approach is compassion. This is the next strongest way to purify negativity.

In the practice of Vajrasattva, we feel the presence of an embodiment of wisdom and compassion. First we feel it to be 'out there' and then we bring the feeling 'in here' [indicating the heart area, the body]. When we visualise Vajrasattva above our head, we project the qualities of wisdom and compassion 'out there.' This might seem a funny thing to do, but actually we are always projecting 'out there.' We are very good at projecting and do it most of the time. Even, for example, falling in love is actually a projection. That is why people fall in love typically under moonlight, or candlelight - because then you can't see so well, so you can project anything!

Here we project positive qualities so that we can learn to experience and generate them. We focus our entire mind on the visualisation, our whole thinking and emotional mind is absorbed in feeling loving-kindness and compassion and wisdom, and also the energy of healing. Our whole mind is occupied in this, instead of our usual way of focusing on problems and negative things. So, we are learning a new habit, we are creating a new habitual tendency.

Vajrasattva visualisation

You visualise Vajrasattva above the crown of your head, not sitting directly on top of your head but a little way above. You visualise a lotus flower and, on top of that, a moon disc – a flat disc the colour of the moon. This symbolises purity and 'coolness.' Then you feel that Vajrasattva is inseparable with the lineage and your guru. He is white in colour, symbolising being pure and untainted.

He is decorated like a prince, with ornaments and clothes of silk and so on, symbolising that there is nothing to get rid of, no penance needed – there is no need to bear hardships or anything like that, to pay penance for anything. There is nothing like that; it is already done and completed. There is nothing to purify. Everything is complete. So he does not need to be like an ascetic, someone trying to get rid of something. He has already done it. There is nothing more to purify; he is totally free.

The thangka picture in the front of the book is done in the Tibetan style. It was painted by my brother, Salga. But if you have any problem with how it looks, if it feels culturally distant or anything, you don't have to visualise in that way. You can see Vajrasattva any way you like. The main thing is the concept of a totally enlightened being, with limitless compassion and limitless wisdom. Nothing more to get rid of: totally accomplished, and so adorned with all the positive qualities, represented by the ornaments.

Then, Vajrasattva is sitting crossed-legged; one hand holding the vajra and one hand holding the bell, like in the image. The vajra symbolises indestructibleness. Vajra is sometimes translated as 'diamond' but it is not just a diamond. There is a legend about the vajra: Once the king of heaven, Indra, was about to be defeated by lots of negative forces, so he called all the rishis [wise men or hermits] and asked, 'What can we do? The positive side is losing to the negative forces, because they are so strong now.'

And the rishis replied, 'You have to get the vajra. The vajra is an indestructible weapon that can destroy anything but cannot be destroyed by anything.'

So, Indra asked, 'Where is the vajra?'

'It can only be made from the bones of a highly realised rishi. His flesh should be licked clean by a red cow and then the bones that are left will become the vajra. You have to go and ask him if he will give you this.'

So, Indra went and found this highly realised rishi. And, as he was sitting in front of him, the rishi asked, 'What do you want?'

'I need the vajra,' said Indra.

'But where is the vajra? I don't have any vajra,' said the rishi.

'But you *are* the vajra – your bones are the vajra! We are in a very difficult situation. The negative forces are becoming stronger and stronger. So, I am here to ask if you will give your bones for the vajra.'

So, the rishi said, 'Okay, yes, bring the red cow.'

They brought the red cow and his bones were licked clean and became the vajra. So that is the legend. But what it symbolises is something that is impregnable. It can destroy anything but it cannot be destroyed by anything. That is the vajra.

The essence of our mind is also the vajra. Emptiness is also the vajra. When we understand the way that things really are, we can become free from all fear and clinging. So, therefore, we attain the vajra state, through that understanding. We know that there is nothing here that can be destroyed. We are indestructible because we are emptiness. When I understand that, I get the vajra. That is the real vajra and the symbol of this is a ritual object which is called a vajra, made of metal, which you can see the design of in the picture. Vajrasattva holds this in his right hand.

Then, in his left hand Vajrasattva holds a bell. The bell is a symbol of interdependence: When you ring a bell, where is the sound? There is ringing, but the bowl of the bell is not the ringing, the clanger of the bell is not the ringing, my ear is not the ringing, the air is not the ringing sound. So, where is the sound? The sound is something you cannot hold on to, you cannot pin it down. But when all these things are there, the sound happens. And you cannot destroy it. It is an interdependent arising. Everything that is interdependently arising is like that: it is there but it is not there. Therefore, you cannot hold onto it and you cannot destroy it. It changes; it disappears; it comes again; when all the conditions are there, then it appears.

Vajrasattva is the representation of that. The Vajrasattva *is* bell and *dorje* [Tibetan for vajra]. Vajrasattva is having that understanding of yourself. When you understand yourself like that, then you have attained Vajrasattva. You have learnt how to purify yourself.

To begin with, when we do not have that level of understanding or experience, then we can use this practice to help us. We can see Vajrasattva as a Buddha and we can make a request or say prayers to make a connection with Vajrasattva. We cultivate devotion to Vajrasattva and we invoke his blessings. And so we say his mantra.

As the text says:

'Clearly visualise at Vajrasattva's heart centre a moon disc, upon which sits a HUM, encircled by the mantra garland.'

You can practise drawing the *HUNG* [or *HUM*] that is in the centre of Vajrasattva's heart, to become familiar with it. The whole mantra is like a garland around the *HUNG*. It is very small and shining, clear and white. This is also a meditation because, when you visualise something very small like this, bright and shining and clear, you are training your mind to focus on it, clearly and at the same time in a very relaxed way. So you are training your mind to be focused and clear but not in a tight way.

'Due to your supplicating him, a stream of amrita fills his body and descends from his right big toe, entering the Brahma aperture at the top of your head.'

Because of your devotion and prayers, you feel that cleansing or purifying amrita. It is like a cooling, cleansing liquid and it fills up the body of Vajrasattva and flows out of his right big toe and enters through your fontanel. You feel that, inside your body, everything is purified and cleaned.

'All your obscurations and past negative actions, embodied in a substance that looks like ink or dark smoke, leave your body as all of your body's parts are filled with amrita. While doing this visualisation, recite Vajrasattva's mantra as many times as you can.'

So, this is the main practice. You feel that the amrita or cleansing nectar enters into your body. You feel good about that. You feel comfortable, happy, warm. All the negative things that are inside you, all the diseases in your body, all the negative emotions you have, all the negative habitual tendencies that you hold onto in your body, everything is cleaned and taken off from you, in the form of something like dirt. It is washed out of you. You feel totally cleaned and purified and transformed. You not only have no more pain or illnesses in you, but you also have no more negative feelings or emotions.

Then you feel free of all the negative things. They are washed off in the form of something like a dark smoke. And your body is filled with amrita. You feel joyful, and completely healed and transformed. Once all the impurities have left you, you feel that the amrita fills you up, from your base up to the crown of your head. You can go through this visualisation one time in a session, or many times.

Feeling all that positivity, rather than focusing on the negative things, you recite the mantras. There are two mantras: the hundred-syllable mantra and the six-syllable mantra. So, you do the hundred-syllable mantra as much as you can and then you do the six-syllable mantra, also.

These mantras can be pronounced in different ways, but one way Tibetans traditionally say them is:

OM BENZA SATO SAMAYA MANUPALAYA / BENZA SATO TENOPA / TISHTA DRI DHO MEBHAWA / SUTO KAYO MEBHAWA / SUPO KAYO MEBHAWA / ANURAKTO MEBHAWA / SARWA SIDDHI MEMTRAYATSA / SARWA KARMA SUTSA ME TSITTAM SHIRIYA KURU HUNG / HA HA HA HA HO BHAGAWAN / SARWA TATHAGATA / BENZA MAME MUNTSA / BENZA BHAWA / MAHA SAMAYA SATO AH

And:
OM BENZA SATO HUNG

Completion

At the end of saying mantras, you say the closing words.

'Then, confess your past negative actions and vow not to perform them again by reciting the following:

Noble ones who know and see everything, think of us.
Since beginningless time,
Under the power of the three poisons,
We have transgressed the three vows and the victors' commands
In body, speech and mind.
We admit and confess these downfalls and misdeeds
And promise not to do them again – may we not experience
their results.'

When it says 'Noble ones,' it means highly realised beings like Buddhas, omniscient beings. 'Think of us' is the translation but it is very hard to translate the Tibetan into English here. It is not just 'think of us' but there is no other way of saying it, except something like 'give attention to us.' 'Since beginningless time' means we don't know since when, we don't know the start. Since time immemorial, we have been under the influence of our three poisons: ignorance, aversion and attachment. Under the power of these, we have done lots of negative things. We have done things we vowed not to do and things we are not supposed to do.

One of the names of the Buddha is *Jina* which is translated here as 'victor.' *Jina* means 'the one who has overpowered' all the negative, and has therefore become the victor. So, the 'victors' commands' means, not exactly the commands, but all the teachings of all the Buddhas.

We confess these downfalls, as it says, but it means more than just 'confess.' 'Confess' in English means 'to say or to acknowledge' that what I have done is wrong. There is an accepting that what I have done is

wrong and I do not want to do it again. This is part of purification –
acknowledging a negative deed to be negative is the beginning of your
purification. Confessing is saying that and that you want to let go of it.
But the Tibetan word used here, *Shagpa* (pronounced *shakpa*), does not
only mean to do this. It includes this meaning but it also means 'to get rid
of, to let go, to purify' these negative things. *Shag* literally means to cut or
cleave, like splitting a log with an axe. One part is cut away from the other
part. So, *Shagpa* means to completely separate, to dissociate, to cut away.

So, I let go of all my downfalls and misdeeds. 'Misdeeds' mean doing
whatever is not good to do. 'Downfalls' are when I promised to do
something good but I did the opposite. And I promise not to do it again
because if I do something negative, and I do it knowingly, again and
again, it's not good for me. I vow not to do anything negative and I don't
hold on to anything negative. So then, I ask that I may not experience
the result of anything I have already done.

'Saying this, confess and resolve not to repeat your misdeeds.'

We say this with a strong kind of a resolution that we let go of all these
negative things. When we are talking about negative things here, it
means not only negative things that *I have done*, but also negative things
that *I have experienced,* anything that is negative that I have experienced.
This is anything that has been done to me, that I kind of hold on to,
whether in my body, in my speech or in my mind. Any habitual
tendencies towards that, I allow them to go. Whatever has happened,
we can still have the attitude, 'It happened, it is done, and now I don't
want to hold on to any habitual tendencies in body, speech and mind
because of it, so I let it go.'

At this point then, I feel that Vajrasattva says, 'Your misdeeds are
purified, done, finished.' And you feel that you have been able to let
them go. This is important – this is the practice. The practice is that you
actually *feel* that they are gone.

Then the Vajrasattva melts into light and dissolves into you. Right from the beginning Vajrasattva is made of light and is not so solid. Now it melts into light and enters into me through my crown. I feel that I have myself become as pure as Vajrasattva, as enlightened as Vajrasattva. There is no difference between us. The essence of my mind is no different from Vajrasattva.

What is the essence of my mind? It is awareness. There is knowingness, awareness, and then nothing else. Because if we ask, for example, 'What is the shape of my mind?' Nobody can say, because it is not there. 'What is the colour of my mind?' Nobody can say. Then it is not there. There is nothing called 'mind' anywhere that anybody can say 'this is your mind.' There is no shape, no form, no substance, nothing. There is just awareness and that is the mind.

When there is nothing there, you cannot cut it, you cannot destroy it. You cannot destroy something that is not there. So, therefore, your mind is indestructible, in a way. The only thing you can see or feel is the awareness. So it is pure from the beginning. There is nothing that is impure. There is nothing actually wrong with it. The wrong thing is our way of reacting and experiencing. We think we see something there that is very tangible and that it is very destructible. So we have lots of fear and feel we need to protect it. But what is it that we are seeing?

The body – it is changing anyway. I can never protect it, it will go. The moment I am born it is starting to decay. It is changing all the time. However I try, I cannot protect it. Every day, it is changing. Every moment, even, it is changing. Death is not one thing that happens in one moment. It is not like *'Now* there is death,' whereas before there was no death at all. We sometimes see it like this but actually every day is a death. Every evening is like a death. Every morning is like a birth. And every moment is like that. Things are changing all the time. So, therefore, there is nothing I can do to protect my body eventually.

My mind – there is nothing that can actually happen to it because there is nothing there. So having lots of fear and worry is useless. When I understand this deeply, then I am free. Then I can relax. I can become Vajrasattva. When I become him, I see my awareness and Vajrasattva are the same thing. I can relax in that and rest in that – in total relaxation. No need to fear. No need to run after. No need to run away. Just relax.

So, then you remain in that feeling of being inseparable from Vajrasattva as long as possible:

'Rest in equipoise.'

Post-meditation

This now is really the main practice. We are not necessarily always visualising Vajrasattva. Sometimes we might visualise Vajrasattva but sometimes there is no need to. You can forget the visualisation and just directly practise as below.

'Second, between sessions, whatever afflictions or thoughts arise, be mindful of them as soon as they arise.'

'Afflictions' mean negative emotions and things like that which arise, or just simple thoughts might arise. You are aware of what is happening: you are clear and aware that this emotion is happening or this reaction is happening or this thought is arising. You are aware of it and mindful.

'Completely cut through them and rest in freedom from fixation.'

This is the practice. Usually when there are emotions, or thoughts and concepts, happening, either we follow them, hold on to them and become a slave of them, or we are afraid of them and we try to get rid of them. We try to run away from them. Neither is necessary - because we cannot do either. So what we need to do is cut through them and just let it happen: 'This thought is happening, or this emotion is happening – *okay*.' We neither follow it, nor become averse to it. We cut through it. If you cut something, then you are not holding on to it. You rest in freedom from fixation. You don't fixate; so, therefore, you are free. If anything happens, let it be like the wind blowing straight through, in one window and out of another. Let it come and let it go. This means you are not fixating. You are not trying to stop it. You are not following it. You are not becoming overpowered by it. You let it through. That is cutting through.

When you can do that, then you have learned how to self-liberate your thoughts and emotions. 'Self-liberate' means you don't need to do something to liberate it. It is liberated by itself. When it is liberated by itself, you are not bound, you are free. This is something very important to know about. It is not easy to learn and not easy to do at this point. But this is really the key. This is how we rest in freedom from fixation.

> *'Whatever sentient beings you see, hear or think of – especially those who have done terrible misdeeds – visualise Vajrasattva above their heads and recite the hundred-syllable mantra.'*

This is how you try to help others. If you see somebody, even a very negative person who has done lots of bad things, you see Vajrasattva above their head and do the same practice as you have done with yourself. You feel they are being purified. You try to see everybody as becoming transformed, pure. You not only learn to see yourself as pure but also learn to see everybody as pure.

Setting the Practice in Context

There are two different things relating to a practice: one is what is called the *sadhana*, or the formal practice, and the other is working with it in a wider context. The *sadhana* is a kind of ritual or text or method that we try to follow. But this needs to be understood in a bigger context: we have to understand the essence of the practice. Otherwise, it can become like a tradition or ritual that is only performed as a ritual and is nothing more: 'I only do it because I am following a tradition.' Then it will not work.

It is, therefore, very important to understand the whole context and why we are doing a certain practice. For example, 'By doing this, I am working on this kind of a problem or that kind of an improvement.' The more we understand like this, the more the practice is a true practice. Then it never becomes just a ritual or a tradition, followed hollowly.

So, now we will look at some of the wider aspects that should be understood in association with Vajrasattva practice. The problem here, however, is that in Buddhism it is very difficult to find a good place to start, somewhere that really provides a good beginning for any explanation, because all the topics are so inter-related. They depend on each other to understand the whole approach, so it can very quickly become not very much of a 'beginning' style.

I think many people have found this about Buddhism. To find a book that is really on the basics, and gives them very clearly, is difficult. I tried myself to write one, but it is very difficult. If you start with the Four Noble Truths, it soon becomes complicated. If you start with Refuge, again, it is not really the beginning. Whatever you start with, it is like that. But let us look here at the three sacred principles.

Three sacred principles

Sometimes people call this:

- Good in the beginning
- Good in the middle
- Good in the end

First, one generates a positive motivation, one corrects or clears the aspiration.

Then, the next thing is the actual practice – to understand the actual practice, and not become too obsessed or dogmatic about it: to understand it with a little bit of selflessness. When I say selflessness, it is not about saying, 'I am not there.' Selflessness means there is nothing that is there, on its own, independently. Everything is an interdependently-arising thing. So, practice is too, and has to be understood in that way. That means you do it in a little bit of a relaxed way, not too much grasping or being dogmatic about it. You bring a little bit of understanding emptiness into it.

Third, is then the dedication. Whatever practices we do or good deeds we perform, whatever good results we get from anything we do or see or experience, whatever we have accomplished, we don't hold on to any of this. We learn how to let all these go. We give them away. We learn how to share them. This is the dedication.

Motivation

These three aspects make up the whole of practice. They start with the motivation, which is the 'why' I do this. Why do I do anything? To ask that question, creates the motivation. It is not as simple as it looks – it is a big question. When we look deeply into our heart, what is it that we really wish? It might not be very difficult to find that we want to be free of what we, in Buddhism, call suffering. I don't want anything bad. I don't want pain and problems, mental problems as well as physical problems. I don't want anything to go wrong. This is what the word 'suffering' denotes.

I don't know what the word 'suffering' means to you. Of course, a word is just a symbol, a sound symbol, so you can put any meaning to it. The meanings of words change all the time. When a Buddhist says 'suffering,' it is usually the translation of *Duhkha* in Sanskrit (*Dukkha* in Pali). *Duhkha* means anything 'not nice,' anything from a little bit of dissatisfaction through to really big mental and physical pain. All of this is included in the term, from the smallest to the biggest lack of comfort, dissatisfaction, problems and pain. It is what we do not want. Nobody wants that. We want the opposite: we want complete happiness, complete satisfaction, complete joy, complete well being for ourselves.

However, if we look a little bit deeper, we find that if I have no problem for myself, it is not enough. Because there are people that I love and, if they have a problem, then I have a problem too. There is nobody who does not have some connection or relationship or love or friendship. So, therefore, wanting to be free from suffering, myself only, is not the solution; it is not the end of the problem. I need to think about others also, not only myself. And how extended that feeling goes, is different for different people. If you are very selfish, then it does not go far. If you are less selfish, then it goes a little bit further.

Then, your loved ones have their loved ones too. It is all very interdependent. Somebody was saying to me that there was a calculation showing that any two people on this earth, however far or distant they are from each other, would have a mutual friend or acquaintance within seven people. Nobody is so far away from each other, in a way. Also, things affect each other. So, it is illogical to only be concerned for oneself. It is not because you 'have to be compassionate' or that it is 'the Buddhist way' or even that it is 'a good thing to do.' It is simply logical; if others are not free from suffering, I cannot be either. Whether we like it or not, we are connected. We are not connected with a chain but interdependently and dependently other people's state of being affects my well being. So, there is no way I can avoid having to do something for the good of *some* other people, at least. And the more people included, the better it is.

We can say, therefore, it is a fact that we need to wish good things for others as well as for ourselves, for both ourselves and others to be free from suffering. It is necessary to have a good wish for everybody, to have a genuine benevolent aspiration for others and myself. The more I have that, the more I feel 'whole' and I feel more useful. We have a kind of instinctive wisdom, which means if we think or feel in a certain way, we feel good, or in another way, we feel bad. We know somewhere inside. When we feel a positive benevolent feeling to everybody, we feel genuinely good. If a person is feeling they are doing something good, they will generally not feel 'wrong.' But if somebody has a negative wish or a malevolent feeling towards somebody, then they will generally not feel very good about that; they know something is wrong.

This positive feeling and benevolent aspiration is, itself, a direct experience of well being. It is not that if you have good wishes and Bodhicitta, then one day you will do something good and then some time after that you will get something good. The moment you feel this benevolent feeling towards beings, you immediately have this experience of feeling more joyful, more peaceful and more serene. *That itself* is an experience of peace: undisturbed, tranquil, maybe even warmth. It brings peace and satisfaction itself.

The more you feel this, the more it will bring forth positive actions of your body, mind and speech. Positive actions naturally follow this positive aspiration. You do not have to try or make a special effort; when you really feel positive and kind, then whatever you say will come out nicely. And whatever you do will also be nice; even your body language will show it. Even if nobody understands your language where you are, they will know you are meaning well. It permeates out.

This is something, therefore, that we should try to generate. We should exercise ourselves on it and learn how to generate it. Sometimes people say, 'Why should I be nice to others? They are not nice to me!' It is not about that; it is not about 'tit for tat.' If I am not nice because they are not nice, they will be even more not nice, and then so will I, and we will end up with a very strong conflict. This attitude simply does not lead to anything good; it gives no solution.

It does not mean, however, that I have to be 'heavy' on myself about feeling compassionate. I do not have to be like a doormat. I do not have to do everything people ask me to do. I do not have to be like a slave and unable to ever say or do anything bad. It is not that I cannot even think anything bad – 'I want to think bad things... but I can't!' That way does not work either. It just builds resentment. This is not what the teaching means. It is not that you have to be obsequious and overly nice to everybody. It is not that you have no say in what you do. You can always say 'no' to anybody.

You are responsible for yourself. If someone else wants you to do something, you can decide whether you want to do it or you do not want to do it. You decide whether it is good for you and for others, or if it is not good for you and for others. If you decide it is good for you and for others, then why not do it? Even if they do not ask you to, you can do it. If it is not good for you and for others, then it is not good to do it, even if they ask you to.

You do not have to succumb to the pressure of everybody. Having a good intention does not mean that. It does not mean you have to please everybody. Nobody can please everybody. It is sometimes not good to please people. People are not necessarily always wise. So, therefore, if they ask you to do something that is not good for them or for yourself, and then they get angry if you don't do it, what can you do? You should still not do it. If they get angry, okay, let them.

When we talk about a positive aspiration or good intention, therefore, it does not mean just to please people. I have the right to decide what is good and what is not good – I *must* have that right. It is up to me to think about it. I have to be responsible for my actions. I can decide. But I do not need to have bad intentions. I do not need to wish bad to anybody. If somebody does not like me, I can still wish him or her well. If somebody likes me, I can wish him or her well, too.

I do not need to have bad wishes even to somebody who tries to harm me, because this kind of thing happens, and it happens all the time. Enemies can also turn into friends. Nothing is permanent. The worst enemy can become your best friend sometimes. Or sometimes what looked like somebody trying to harm me can turn out to be good for me. Or sometimes I might be harmed but, even then, wishing bad or getting too negative myself is not good for me.

When we say to have a benevolent feeling towards everybody, it is not to say that you do not understand clearly whatever is going on. It is not to say that everybody will be nice and kind to you if you have a positive and benevolent feeling yourself. Of course, the more you have a benevolent feeling, the more likely it is that people will react similarly to you. But it is not guaranteed that people will respond in the same way. But, if I have a benevolent feeling and somebody tries to harm me, if I feel very angry and upset and negative about that, it does not help me. I was already harmed and now I am harming myself more by allowing myself to be so affected by that.

If I can feel benevolent towards even those who try to harm me, it will be better for me. Of course, I have to do whatever I can to avoid being harmed, but I do not need to take it in a very emotional way. The less anger and upset I have, the better off I am. At least then I do not have layers and layers of pain. If I am not too upset by what I received, I become saner. If I get harmed and feel really bad about it, that can become worse and worse until I get so affected I get into a mental problem, a kind of emotional shock. That is then much worse.

This is the understanding: Nobody can totally harm you, unless you harm yourself. If anybody tries to harm you, you cannot prevent that completely. You cannot force people not to do those things, because what people do and do not do is not under our control. But how much effect it has, is in our area of control. It is not necessary that we have to feel hatred or totally negative feelings. It is much better to feel benevolent. And it is good for me *now*, good for me in the next moment, good for me the next moment, good for me all the time. It is good for others also. Therefore, I need to generate this feeling, and I need to exercise on that.

This background understanding is very important because, without this, if you just try to not feel angry when you are already feeling angry, you can create more problems. You cannot just stop a feeling if it is there. You cannot just stop your emotions. Your emotions come from your way of seeing things. That is where emotions arise from. So, if you have a good and clear understanding that you do not need to feel this way, then you can work on ridding yourself of feeling like that. You can work on your habitual tendencies once you see that it is not necessary to react in that way.

If I can change my way of seeing, I can change my way of feeling. We have to remind ourselves of this understanding often. We have to have the understanding, but also the discipline to allow the positive to come out. And whenever the negative or bad feelings come up, you need to have the diligence and the patience and the discipline to remind yourself of this, and allow that feeling or thought or emotion to let go. This is purification.

Purification has to reach here. The practice has to be done in this way. You can use a method to help yourself let go. There are many things you can do here. For example, you can feel the presence of Vajrasattva and feel the compassion and energy of purification and allow your mind to be in that state. That is the method. The whole idea, once you have this understanding, is to allow *this present moment's* thoughts and emotions to let go, whenever they are negative.

How do I let go of negative thoughts and emotions of this present moment? By allowing something else to come in. What would that be? Let us say, for example, I feel upset because something happened and I am thinking about how upset I am. I want to let go of my upset but my mind is so occupied by it, it is impossible for me to let go of it. It is occupying my mind and my mind is totally full of that problem.

Now, if instead I say, 'Okay, that is there,' the upset, but then I think about Vajrasattva, or Buddha, I can let my mind become totally occupied with that instead. Maybe there is a nice picture of Buddha I can look at and just let my mind become absorbed in the beautiful smile of Buddha, or his very pleasant, very kind face. Then what happens? As long as I am doing that, the upset is not there. I have let go of it. That is the method.

You use this method, becoming absorbed in the feeling of a very beautiful, very kind, very wise being. Then, if seeing the smiling face is not enough, you can also feel radiating lights coming, or nectar cleansing you on the inside. When you are doing that, at least for that moment, you have allowed the upset to go. Then, it is true that our mind is changing very quickly most of the time, so things can change quickly when you stop holding onto something.

Sometimes, I can be very upset and angry about something. If I immediately reacted or replied, I would say very nasty things. But if I delay my response, maybe overnight or even just for ten minutes, the way I react would be very different. For example, I heard that one of the American Presidents used to keep many letters he had written, overnight, so he could see how they looked the next morning, before he sent them. Later on, when he retired, they found a big bundle of letters written to his Generals, really nasty letters, which he never sent.

It is the same with ourselves, also. Except it is more dangerous nowadays, because we have email; it is instantaneous! Often, though, if you wait and do not answer immediately, you will send a very different message the next morning. And then, sometimes, if you wait, the next morning the other person will send you a message, 'Yesterday I was very tired....'

So, therefore, we have to allow things to go when they arise, and sometimes things naturally change also. Purification is letting these negative things go. Of course, our habitual tendencies are difficult to eliminate because we have been reacting that way for a long, long time. It is not that we will never get angry, that is not the point. We will get angry. But that is not a problem if you know how to deal with it.

There is a story about Patrul Rinpoche about this. He was a very, very learned lama but he was a little bit eccentric. [See *Riding Stormy Waves* in the *Heart Wisdom series* for a biography of Patrul Rinpoche.] He had only a camp, no monastery or anything. One day, a lama came to see him and said, 'Ah, I have been meditating so well for so many days now, I have done away with all my anger! I have no more anger.'

Patrul Rinpoche wanted to tease him a little bit. So, after the lama left, Patrul Rinpoche said to somebody, 'This lama says he has done away with all his anger but actually he is not very clean with his hands – he steals sometimes.' So, the rumour spread all round the camp – and a lama stealing is a very bad thing.

Finally, the lama himself heard the rumour and thought to himself, 'I may not be that great, but at least I don't steal! Where is this totally baseless allegation coming from?' He was trying to find the source of the rumour and when he found out it was Patrul Rinpoche himself, he was very angry. He rushed into the Rinpoche's tent and demanded to know why he had said that, really very angrily.

Patrul Rinpoche just laughed and said, 'I thought that you had done away with your anger?' So, then the lama understood.

It shows that it is not easy to do away with anger and other negative emotions. But the point is not about doing away with them, it is about learning how to deal with them. If we can learn how to deal with them, how to let them go, then they do not matter. When you know how to deal with negative emotions, they are no longer negative. They are no longer a big problem.

So, this is mainly about the first aspect of practice, our motivation. Now we will look at the second aspect, what the practice actually is.

Taming your mind

Buddha gave the following advice, which actually includes all the things to do:

'Do no evil.
Try to do positive things as much as possible.
And then, tame your mind.'

We need to start by being a little bit aware of our actions - of body, speech and mind - which includes our thoughts and emotions. If we find we are doing something that brings harm, pain or problems, to myself or others, now or in the long run; that is negative. Whatever I am doing, I need to be aware if my actions are something positive or negative. When you see it is negative, you allow it to be replaced. If you find your action is good, positive and beneficial, then you encourage yourself to do it. You allow yourself to do it and encourage yourself to do it more and strengthen it.

This is taming your mind. When you cannot stop yourself doing something negative, because you are totally overpowered by strong emotions, that is where we need to bring this taming of the mind to. You need to be able to check the flow of your strong emotions and thoughts, and change them mid-stream. This is what all the training is for, including discipline, meditation, and attention. Our mind is all over the place and we cannot bring it together.

I need to bring mindfulness to allow my mind to focus. Most meditation is for this: how to not become totally out of control; how to relax my mind; how to focus my mind; how to change from one thing to another. This is very important. In this particular method, all the visualisation is for that; to learn how to focus your mind.

Sometimes, you can focus on the seed syllable *HUNG,* for example. You let your mind rest on a glowing letter *HUNG,* the colour of the moon, and a little bit complicated. It is good that it is a little bit complicated, because it keeps your mind more awake and alert. Your mind gets more focused when it has to do something a little bit complicated. Also, sometimes, a small image is helpful. So you make the *HUNG* very, very tiny, because the smaller your focus, the sharper your mind will be and you cannot have other things in your mind. They say the *HUNG* can be as if written by one strand of a hair; shiny, clear and distinct, but very small. And sometimes you can make it big, instead.

They don't talk about this so much, but actually it is very important to change your focus when you visualise something. Sometimes, you focus on the whole body of the Vajrasattva. Sometimes, you are not focussing on the whole body, but on the whole environment – very spacious and beautiful, a palace and a lake and so on. Sometimes, you just focus on the face or on one hand. And sometimes, you can focus on an even smaller area, like the *HUNG* in the heart.

Sometimes you focus on something that is static, like the lotus flower or the form of Vajrasattva. Sometimes you focus on something moving, like radiating lights or the feeling of being purified. You can focus on all the beings and also on yourself. This is important to change your focus, because when you become a little bit tired or dull or unfocused with one thing, you can change to something else.

Student: You mean you change your focus within one session?

Rinpoche: Yes, definitely, even within a few minutes. It is not that you have one thing that is like a statue and that is it. That is why all the different aspects of a visualisation are described. It is not necessary to focus on everything at once, but you can change your focus from time to time, so you do not get tired or sleepy.

All these things are to train our mind. This is actually all Shamatha meditation but there are different methods of Shamatha. In any Buddhist practice the meditation will be either Shamatha or Vipashyana. The meditation to train your mind is basically Shamatha. We also have the cultivation of compassion and wisdom, and Vipashyana is more about wisdom.

Wisdom and compassion

Generally speaking, everything is about wisdom and compassion. In order to generate these, you train on how to lessen your negative deeds, how to enhance your positive deeds and then how to train your mind. Compassion is the motivation and is within the practice too. In the practice, we see not only myself being purified, but every being. This is compassion in action; allowing everybody to be purified. Every being is within your mind; you are putting them all in the same boat as yourself. This is also working on compassion.

When we try to describe wisdom, we often talk about the nature of the mind or the nature of phenomena, interdependence and emptiness, all these things. This is wisdom but wisdom is also – and I think this is a major part of wisdom – about learning how to deal with anything. It is learning how to experience things in a proper way.

What is a wise person anyway? A wise person is not necessarily a scholar; he or she can be a scholar but not necessarily. A wise person is not necessarily always popular. They do not necessarily have lots of influence on people. They are not necessarily a rich person, either. A wise person is somebody who knows how to deal with any situation.

So, wisdom can come through these understandings and through these practices, so that we learn how to deal with our thoughts and our emotions and our experiences. When we can do this, and there is no problem for us, that is when we have found wisdom. It is not an intellectual understanding. It is an experiential understanding. If you are able to give a long commentary on emptiness, that is very good but you are not necessarily wise. You may be learned but still not wise. Wisdom is about knowing how to experience things.

All these things are within this practice, which appears at first to be quite simple. You have to know that they are in there, so you can bring them out. Once you know how to use this practice to work on all these things, then you really have a practice. Then, with just the practice of Vajrasattva, you can become enlightened! You do not need any other practice. And you can do any other practice in the same way. It is just the form that is different, but the form is not the important thing.

The main thing is understanding it is a practice, which means it is a method to work on yourself, and understanding how it does that. Once you have this core understanding, then maybe exactly how you see Vajrasattva, or how you pronounce the mantra, does not matter so much. For example, some people might have an accent or a way of speaking that means they cannot say the words exactly how they are usually said. This does not stop that person being able to accomplish the practice.

Transforming klesha and karma

When we talk about practice to work on ourselves, we are talking about transforming ourselves. What is it that we want to transform? What is it that all the suffering and problems are coming from? First we see that, we recognise that. From the Buddhist point of view, the most important things that make us suffer and bring problems again and again, for ourselves and others, are the kleshas and karma.

Klesha is the Sanskrit word that is sometimes translated as 'disturbing emotion.' And sometimes it is translated as 'mind poison.' However you translate it, it means the state of mind that consists of what we call negative emotions: like anger, hatred, greed, jealousy and pride, and also misunderstandings and doubts. It means the states of mind which create unpleasantness and 'un-peacefulness.' The states of mind which bring anguish, which bring tension, which bring sadness, which bring fear, those kind of negative emotions.

When they become a little bit strengthened, the negative emotions then become negative habitual tendencies and those then give rise to negative actions. The actions that come out of these negative emotions create problems for others and for ourselves. This then is karma. Karma comprises all our actions and reactions, not only those made with our body and speech, but also with our mind. Mostly it is the emotions, and the actions coming out of them, which create painful experiences for ourselves and others.

These two things, the kleshas and karma, are regarded as the pain, the problem, as the source of things. And if we look a little bit more deeply into why we have these negative emotions, what we find is that it is due to ignorance. We don't see what is the best way to react to a certain situation. We don't know how to experience something, whatever happens, so we experience it in a bad way. So, then, these negative emotions come and because of these, negative reactions and habitual tendencies also come.

If you go down the path of this way of reacting then it is described as reacting with aversion and attachment. Generally, we react in one of three ways. Whatever we see or come into contact with through the five senses, then we say either 'This is nice' or 'This is not nice' or we just ignore it. If we just ignore it, that's another matter, but if we react, then we react either that it is nice, too nice, or it is bad.

It is not to say that we should not see good things and bad things. We have to see them. That is no problem. But our reaction becomes a little bit too strong or too much. It is not enough to say, 'This is nice.' Because the moment you say, 'This is nice,' you say, 'I want it.' 'I want to have it.' The nicer you see it as, the more you want to get it, the more you want to have it and the more you become unhappy if you don't get it.

So, if I see a nice flower I can say, 'Oh, this is a nice flower.' I can enjoy that - that is okay. But that is not the way we leave it. 'This nice flower – I want it... I need it... nobody else should have it.' Then I start to think, 'How can I have it?' But even if I get it, it is not perfect because I might lose it. So again, I have problems. And if I lose it, I have more problems. It is like a chain of problems, not because this is nice, not because I appreciate it; but because of my attachment, because I react in a certain way, which is unnecessary.

The other way of reacting is aversion: 'This is not nice.' It is okay, this is just not nice. But we think, instead, 'This is not nice... This should not be here... I must get rid of it... I must not have it.' The more we think like this, the more it brings lots of fear and anger. So, it cannot be like that. If it is there I am unhappy. You know that there can be some things that are not so nice. There can be some things that are there and they are not so nice and it is still okay. But that is not the way we usually react. Something that is not so nice, we exaggerate how we see it until it is really fearsome. We make a big problem out of it. We make a lot of unhappiness for ourselves and create a lot of problems like that.

This aversion brings fear - rejecting something very strongly and trying to run away from it. But we can never run away from it because the fear *is* the aversion. We can be afraid of something even if it is not there. We can have aversion to something that is there but we can also have aversion and fear to something that is not there. So how can we run away from that? We think, 'Oh, something terrible will happen...' Until that happens or until I have no more fear of it, that fear is always there. Therefore, the aversion is very difficult to get rid of. It is actually a way of reacting.

These two things, aversion and attachment, are based on a wrong way of seeing. That is why we say they come from ignorance. This is the basic source of the mind-set which generates all the negative emotions like anger and hatred. Greed also comes from aversion and attachment because we think, 'I want something... I want to get it... I must have it... Something terrible will happen if I do not have it.' It is all aversion and attachment and the more we react with these, the more we act in a negative way. The stronger we do that, the stronger the mental and emotional problems we create and the more unhappy our life is. Therefore, to work on these, aversion and attachment, is the practice. This is where all the problems are coming from.

Letting go of aversion and attachment

We have these two practices to work on aversion and attachment: Vajrasattva practice and Mandala offering. Vajrasattva practice is *basically* for aversion, for fear, for the negative. Purification is that – anything that is what we call negative, that I don't like, that is not nice, that I have or that might happen to me and the causes and conditions that create those negative things - I let go of these. I try not to hold on to them; or rather I exercise myself to do this, rather than 'try.' It is not so much 'I try,' more that 'I just do.'

I *allow* myself to make myself free from anything negative, whether it is my own actions that are negative, my own emotions that are negative, my habitual tendencies or anything that is there that might cause me pain and suffering, like negative deeds or negative influences. Anything that is not so nice, I let it go. I feel free from that. I let go of the aversion, the fear.

We do it again and again, this exercise of letting go, because we are working on our habitual tendencies. We have a very strong tendency to hold on to negative things. That is our problem actually – we hold on to negative things. Maybe something negative happened to us even a long time ago but it is still very difficult to let it go. We think things like, 'If I make even one mistake, it will happen again...' But actually everything changes, nothing remains, everything changes all the time. Yesterday is gone. The only thing that remains of yesterday is that we remember. We cannot get yesterday back – unless we go in a time machine! - which anyway doesn't exist, so far. But even if we went in a time machine, I don't think we can really experience yesterday again: it's just a concept. We can't experience it because it is not there anymore. What is gone, is gone. It is not there.

We hold on to all those things, from a long time ago. Even one word said by somebody, not so nice, we keep it for the whole of our life. Why? It creates lots of problems, but still we keep hold of it. Or something happened to me in my childhood or my youth, and I keep it all my life. It influences my whole life. It is very difficult to let go of negative things, although we don't want them. We are not supposed to want the negative things but we somehow cannot let go.

There is a Buddhist anecdote, about somebody who was in hell. This person was suffering all these things horrible things, like boiling oil - hell is not a nice place, is it? He had been there for a long, long time and had come to his time to leave. As he was going out of hell, he called back, 'Don't let anybody sit on my seat!' You don't really want to reserve a seat in hell. But it becomes like '*my* seat,' even if it is boiling with lava. And that is actually how our habitual tendency becomes. So we really need to practice to do something about it and that is the essence of the Vajrasattva practice: to allow negative things to go.

Negative things that happened to me, *are* not me. Negative things that are done by me, *are* not me. Whatever problems or difficult things or unpleasant things are around me, they change. Even *me*, I am not something that is unchanging. Everything that is there is changing all the time. So there is nothing I can hold on to. There is nothing I can hold on to and yet I try to hold on to things – that is the problem. The problem is actually that I try to hold on to things that I can never hold on to. That is what makes the struggle. I cannot hold on to even good things, or bad things, because everything changes.

That is why they say, in one way, I am like a river. This is a very traditional way to say it. I am a lot of things, an interdependent entity and a flowing, changing entity, like a river. A river is not only one thing, it is lots of water and the water that is there *now* is not there *now*, at the next moment. It is gone. You call the whole thing 'river' because it is a phenomenon, but it is always changing. I am like that. If I was the river and then I was trying to hold on to the riverbanks, it is not possible for me to do. Then the more I try to do that, the worse it becomes. It can't be anything but problematic for me. That is the way it is.

There is no way I can hold on to negative things as well as positive things. It is not possible for me to do it. It is not good for me to do it. But then why do we do it? That is because of our wrong way of seeing. I don't know how to not do that. I don't know how to react. I don't know how to experience myself. That is the problem. In order to change that, I need to learn, and I need to learn in a practical way. It is not just a theory. I can understand theory easily but I cannot understand it practically very easily.

It is like learning to drive a car. In theory, it is very easy. You can be shown, in the car: this is the shift, this is the accelerator and this is the wheel and you just turn it wherever you want to go. If you press the accelerator, it goes fast. If you want to stop, press the brake and it will stop. It is very easy. But if you don't know how to drive, it's very difficult. (I won't tell you how I failed my driving test!) In theory it is very easy – no problem - but in practice it is very difficult. You need to practise it. Some people who know very well how to drive say it is easy – it is like walking, you don't need to make any special effort. But until you get to that point it is very difficult.

This Vajrasattva practice is training, therefore; training to let go of negative things, of aversion. Mandala offering is training to let go of attachment, of positive things. We need to let go of negative as well as positive. Purification is just that. Purification is nothing more than that - just to allow ourselves to let go of anything that is negative. And then if we can do that, we are pure. There is nothing called 'impure' actually - or there is nothing called 'pure' which is purified or clean - because everything is the same. Everything is changing. Everything is momentary. Everything goes and everything is emptiness and interdependent. It is appearing but nothing is remaining. That is not only true of things around us, but for ourselves too.

When I deeply understand that, there is nothing called negative or positive because nothing is very solid. Everything is interdependent. Everything is fluid. Everything is emptiness and arising: appearance and emptiness. Therefore, there is nothing there to hold on to and nothing there that you *can* hold on to. When I understand this, then I can relax and let be. When I can relax and let be, then it is pure. There is nothing to purify.

'To purify' is not that you have something there that is negative and you have to clean it and clean it and clean it and then you have become very clean. That does not make something very pure, because once you have cleaned it, then it will become 'not clean' again. You cannot purify something and then 'become pure.' The true purification is to see that there is nothing that needs to be purified and there is nothing that can be purified. There is nothing that is 'pure,' against 'impure.' It is just one way of your reacting.

We need to change that way of reacting, because that way of reacting, with aversion and attachment, is based on a wrong way of experiencing. It is not necessary to react like that. I need to understand this deeply: that it depends on *my* way of reacting, whether something is nice or not, pure or not pure. Whether I react with aversion and attachment or with a little bit of tranquillity and peace and joy, *is* the way I will become. Therefore, I need to learn how to react in a better way. If there are colourful things I can see, nice things I can see, everything can be nice. Everything is pure. Everything is good.

That is why sometimes in Buddhist meditations the mandala we visualise not only includes nice things, 'pure' things, wonderful things. Sometimes it also includes ugly things, like Vajrakilaya, for example. Vajrasattva is the peaceful form and Vajrakilaya is the wrathful form. Vajrakilaya is the most ugly thing. There is blood and there are dead bodies and rotten heads, half-rotten heads and complete skeletons. There are snakes and all sorts of things like that. That is supposed to be a deity, a mandala – pure.

It is the same whether we visualise that or Vajrasattva, which is supposed to be very beautiful, very youthful and lovely looking. But Vajrakilaya has bumps here and there and is black or blue or blue-green, with blood and pus coming out. The practice is to work on our attachment and aversion. Letting go of all the negative things is the practice of Vajrasattva, and letting go of all the positive things is the practice of Mandala offering.

Questions and Answers

Visualising Vajrasattva

Student: When we visualise Vajrasattva above us, do we see him facing the same way as us or facing towards us?

Rinpoche: You can see Vajrasattva above you facing the same way as you. But if that is not convenient then you can put the visualisation in front of you, facing you, also. The main thing is about the *feeling*, feeling the presence. It is not about too many details of exactly how to see it.

Which mantra?

Student: When do you say the hundred-syllable mantra and when do you say the six-syllable mantra?

Rinpoche: You can alternate them if you like. You can say the hundred-syllable mantra, as many times as you like, and then when you are a little tired of that you can say the six-syllable mantra, maybe for a few malas. And then when you are tired of that you can go back to the hundred-syllable mantra. You can alternate.

Mantras in Sanskrit

Student: In the mantra, is *Benza Sato* the Tibetan and *Vajrasattva* the Sanskrit?

Rinpoche: No, mantras are always in Sanskrit. There is nothing called a

Tibetan mantra. But Tibetans do not know how to pronounce Sanskrit, so sometimes they pronounce it slightly differently. *Benza Sato* is how Tibetans *say* Vajrasattva. In India, and generally, they say mantras should always be said very correctly; otherwise they will not have any power. But it has been proved that it is not exactly so. There are two particular stories:

One is about Atisha Dipamkara, the great Indian pandit. He came to Tibet to revive Buddhism and he had *no* respect for Tibetan mantra recitation, because it is so full of mistakes. But then, one day, he had a very bad throat problem – it was all infected and he could not talk. And someone said, 'Ah, there is a person who does very good mantras and he helps everyone. Let us call him to help.' Atisha was sure he would be no help because his mantra recitation was so full of mistakes, but they called him anyway.

When the man came he was making so many mistakes that in the end Atisha could not control himself any longer and started to laugh out loud. As he did so, the abscess in his throat burst, all the pus came out and, in no time, he was cured!

The other famous story is about the Tibetan lama, Sakya Pandita. He was born in Tibet but as soon as he could speak, he could speak Sanskrit. He knew Sanskrit from birth, although there was nobody to teach him. He became a very great scholar and would make journeys to India. One time he was travelling to India, from Tibet, and he passed a forest. He heard all the trees, the river, everything around, resounding with the sound of mantra – the mantra of Vajrakilaya – but the mantra was slightly wrong.

He thought that there must be a very good practitioner around that area saying mantras, but he was saying them a little bit wrong. He thought, 'I must find the yogi and correct him because, if it is this powerful when they are saying it wrongly, how much better it will be when they say it correctly!'

So, he searched around and found an old yogi in a cave who was saying the mantra. The mantra is supposed to be *OM BENZA KILI KILAYA…* but he was saying, '*OM BENZA CHILI CHILAYA…*' Sakya Pandita went to him and explained the correct mantra pronunciation.

The hermit responded by taking out a wooden peg and, while saying, '*OM BENZA CHILI CHILAYA…*,' he put it into the rock. It went in, as if sliding into mud. He turned and said to Sakya Pandita, 'Now, you do it, with your *KILI KILAYA!*'

I don't know if he did it or not, but Sakya Pandita invited the hermit to accompany him to India, which he did and he also performed miracles there. So, it is better to be correct but, if it is not correct, it is still okay.

Also, though, there is no one way of saying mantras. Even in India, there are slightly different ways of saying the same mantra. So, it depends on what pronunciation you wish to use.

Sound during mantra recitation

Student: When you are doing the silent recitation for any mantra, is it important that there is still a little bit of sound, 'going out into the world?' Or can it be completely silent, only said internally?

Rinpoche: Generally mantras can be said in four different ways: You can sing it, especially if you have a good voice. You can say it loudly so everybody can hear. You can whisper it so you don't disturb other people. Or you can say it in your mind so that it isn't actually heard. These are the four ways. How you would say the mantra depends on the situation and also how you feel. If you have a good voice and you are not disturbing people, then you can sing the mantra. If you are in a group it is very nice to sing it because you also help other people that way. It's good to say it aloud especially if you are a group saying it together. Then if you are alone in your room you can say it aloud or quietly. If you are tired of saying it aloud, you can just say it quietly. And then sometimes, especially if you are doing breathing exercises or something like that, you can just say it in your mind.

Student: And it has as strong an effect whichever way you say it?

Rinpoche: Yes - it is not said that any way has less effect than any other.

Meaning of the mantra

Student: Can you give us your translation of the hundred-syllable mantra, because I have come across different interpretations of it?

Rinpoche: I think many longer texts have a translation given, to give some idea of what the words mean. For example, reading from the Samye Ling text: [2]

"OM

Vajrasattva, by commitment, protect me with your care,
Remain stably present within me.
Lead me to total satisfaction.
Help enable me to develop wholesomely.
Support me with your love.
Bestow all the accomplishments upon me.
Through accomplishing proper activity, may my mind become worthy.
HUNG
HA HA HA HA (the four limitless contemplations)
HO (their joyous play)
Transcendent accomplished Victor,
Embodiment of all the Tathagatas.
May the indestructible never leave me,
May I become a holder of the indestructible.
Such great commitment.
AH"

But, mantras are not very easy to translate. Tantras are very difficult to translate, anyway, because every sentence has four different meanings – at least. And mantras have even more. So, they are not really translatable. Each word has many different levels of meaning and can be explained at many different levels. So, therefore, it is usually not translated and that is why it was not translated into Tibetan. You can translate it but it would not be the same as the original. It would be 'making it very small.' That is why it was not translated.

Of course, you can get something from the word-by-word meaning. But it is not so correct. What I have read out, above, is all in good English, for example. But the Sanskrit is not like that – it is not in clear, proper sentences, because it is pointing to many different meanings. It is not laid out in neat sentences, like prose, or even like poetry. But if you want to get some kind of word meaning then it is more or less like the above. I can't say much more than that.

In a way, it is not so important what the translation of a mantra is. The concept of mantra comes from the idea that if you attain a certain level of realisation or a certain level of knowing how to use the capacity of your mind, then you can transfer your influence or your power to anything. Generally, naturally, the way we are influences things around us. For example, being in a temper: if I am very angry, you can all feel it. If I am very sad, you all feel it. If I am very happy, you all feel it. If I am very kind and compassionate, you also feel that. So we all feel the influence.

Then, it is said, that if I am very strong in something, it can kind of even influence *things* around me also. That's why we talk about blessed places; like Sikkim, for example, is supposed to be blessed. Guru Padmasambhava was here and he said many other great beings were here before him.

The term used here is *dharani*. They say, once you have attained *dharani,* then you have the power to bless things or transfer that power to a word – to one word or more than one word, a mantra. Then anybody can use those words to access that power or that effect. If mantras are created by highly attained beings, they have that power.

Vajrasattva is the embodiment of purification, so the mantra of Vajrasattva has this strong effect of purification. Manjushri is the embodiment of wisdom, the epitome of wisdom. Therefore, if you say the mantra of Manjushri, you connect to wisdom, you increase your wisdom. In the same way, Chenrezig, or Avalokiteshvara, is about compassion. So, the meaning of the mantra is not the most important thing; the influence of it is the most important thing.

Other texts

Student: I have seen the same mantra in other texts, like Green Tara. Is that correct, is it the same one?

Rinpoche: Yes, it is exactly the same. Wherever there is a purification, you put this hundred-syllable mantra.

One hundred peaceful and wrathful deities

Student: I also heard that the hundred syllables stand for all the different aspects of our mind? Is that correct?

Rinpoche: The hundred syllables also stand for one hundred peaceful and wrathful deities. And the hundred peaceful and wrathful deities stand for all our physio-mental states. It can represent many things.

Empowerment

Student: Does one need an empowerment before doing a specific practice, like Mahamudra or Green Tara?

Rinpoche: For Vajrayana or tantra practices, usually empowerment is recommended, because that is like an instruction, a transmission, and a permission to practice. There are lots of practices that do not have, or need, any empowerment. Most of the Sutrayana practices do not have any empowerments, for instance. Vajrayana practices do generally have empowerments and you should get them. But, for instance, there is nothing called a Ngöndro empowerment. If you have the teaching for Ngöndro, that is it, and you can do the practice once you receive the *lung*, the reading transmission.

Working on emotions during the practice

Student: Do we try to work with emotions during the visualisation or do we just focus on the feeling of purity, of cleansing?

Rinpoche: During the practice, you focus on all your negative feelings and emotions being gone, all your pains are gone. This includes what we call the results and the causes. You feel that, with nectar coming down which feels very good and cleansing and warm. You feel that all the bad things are gone away. Sometimes they describe the feeling being like a crystal vase filled with pure milk. You feel fully benevolent, kind, joyful, well, satisfied and pure. You allow that feeling to come through. Then, if a negative feeling comes, you focus on the positive feeling above. Focusing on something positive is the way to prevent negative feelings coming.

We need to learn how to focus, and this we can only learn from practice. It is one of the main things in learning to meditate. You cannot focus in a tight or intense way. You have to be very relaxed and spacious, but maintain a little bit of focus. That is the training that you have to learn, like driving your car. When you are focusing on the face of Vajrasattva, or the seed syllable or the sound of the mantra, other emotions and thoughts do not come too much. If they are there, just let them be and do not focus on them too much. If they are still there, you do the practice again, feeling the cleansing and feeling joyful and kind.

When you feel joyful and kind, usually negative emotions do not come too much. Negative emotions come because you feel frustrated or because you feel fear or dissatisfaction. They come because you are disturbed. So, the less you are disturbed, the more you feel positive and the less negative emotions will come. If negative emotions come, you can also reason with yourself - why do I need to feel like this?

Student: You don't dig around, then, for all your habitual patterns, and try to get them out?

Rinpoche: No, you get all your habitual tendencies out, *altogether.* I don't think you can find one particular habitual tendency, and take it out. Then find another one, and take it out, and so on. There will be no end to it, no? And if you focus too much on that, you are actually making them stronger. You don't need to focus too much on particulars.

Knowing our misdeeds

Student: Do you have to be clear about what you have done that is negative in order to purify it? When the text says, 'I confess all my misdeeds and vow not to repeat them...,' do we have to be clear about what we have done that has been good and what we have done that has not been good? Sometimes things can be mixed, sometimes you do not know if your actions have been good or not.

Rinpoche: If you feel you have done a particular thing that was bad, and it is occupying your mind, then, yes, you can especially focus on that and letting that go. But, otherwise, I do not think you have to find out too much, 'What are all the bad things I have done...?' You do not have to find them all out - and make a long list! You just think that you let go of anything you have done wrong or any negative things you have done, knowingly or unknowingly, and their results.

Negative actions are those actions that are harmful to others or harmful to myself, now or in the long run. But sometimes you do not know which is harmful and which is not. So, then, it is the actions you have done with negative emotions, with anger, with hatred, with greed, with jealousy. If you do any actions, or any reactions you have done, with these strong emotions, those are negative, because they are done with disturbed or negative emotions.

You also let go of anything negative that has happened to you, not only negative things you have done: pains, problems, diseases, any kind of sufferings that you hold on to. You feel that you allow everything to go. You feel cleaned, you feel fresh. You feel you are a new person, without that baggage from the past. That is the feeling of being purified. All your cells are purified and feeling totally new. Actually we are always changing, everything is always moving. But we hold on to the past and say 'this is me.' This is what we have to let go of. Let the past be past.

Purification illness

Student: When you have an illness or strong dreams or something like that, when you are doing an intensive time of practice, like a retreat, could it be the practice taking these things out of you? Like the Vajrasattva practice bringing out an illness, like a purification?

Rinpoche: I don't know. They say that sometimes, if you do a very strong kind of a purification practice, and you have certain illnesses or certain things come up, it is good. They say it is a sign that you are doing good practice, that things are coming out. Generally they say that because we have so much negative karma, we are supposed to have lots and lots of problems for many lifetimes to come. When you are purifying, you can have a little bit of problem, which substitutes all this, and then it is finished. People say that. How true it is, I don't know.

There is another aspect, though. There are teachings that say: if anything negative comes, you should see it as a good thing. This is an important teaching. It is a way of taking happiness and unhappiness onto the path. What we call 'bad' is something that we don't want. And what is 'good' is something that we want. Now, if you *want* something that is bad, it is not bad anymore.

So, if I am sick, and I am very happy that I am sick, then I have what I want and it is not a problem. It is not to say that I have to make myself sick but, if I have sickness, it can be not too bad. It can also be a good thing, because it is a purification. If you can find a way of seeing something desirable in what you have, then your aversion to it becomes less. So, therefore, the suffering it gives you is less and it actually does become something not too bad. That is the secret. Sometimes, if you have a bad thing and you don't mind, it is really not so bad and it goes away very quickly.

Which practice to do

Student: After these two weeks of retreat, when I go home to my normal working life, what would you suggest would be the best practice for me to continue with? If I could commit to, say, two hours a day of practice, should I do the Ngöndro or something like that?

Rinpoche: Two hours a day is a very big commitment. I say this because I am lazy! For some people maybe it is not. But to do something regularly, is very powerful. If you can really do two hours practice every day, it is a very big practice – meaning two hours exclusive practice, not doing other things.

Which particular practice is important for you, is not the same for everybody. Generally, I think the practice you understand most clearly, which you know how it works on you, that is usually the best practice to do. So, that is what you should work on, however long you have for it. One hour or two hours, or even twenty minutes, or fifteen minutes. You should do the practice you really understand how it works.

If you understand, and really connect with the Ngöndro practice, then it is a very good practice. It is a whole practice. There is nothing more than what is included in the Ngöndro. Everything is there, in a way. If you really want to spend two hours a day, then you can do the whole Ngöndro one hundred thousand of each part. That is supposed to be very good. Each part works in a different way, so that is good in itself. It has been said, by great masters many times, that if you really complete the whole Ngöndro once, at least you will never be reborn in a negative realm. So, it is supposed to be very good and powerful for the long run, even if you don't get too many experiences of attainment at the time. That is the general idea.

I think, in our daily practice, we should spend at least some of our time doing a physical practice, like yoga – so we at least do something physical in our practice time each day. In the olden days, everybody used to do lots of physical things. They would cut trees and fetch water and so on. So, there was no need for further exercise and things like that. In Tibet, also, there was not much recommendation to do physical exercises, because this was already a part of everybody's life.

These days, it is not like that anymore. Nobody does anything physical! They go to work by car and then they come back by car. They take the train or the aeroplane. And their work – what you call work – is just sitting on a chair and doing nothing, except maybe making a phone call now and then! So, because there is not too much exercise of the body, I think some physical practice is important for everybody. And also especially some *Pranayama*; I recommend a little bit of that, even if it is just ten minutes or twenty minutes or whatever.

Then, taming the mind meditation: this can be any of many different kinds. Just a simple Shamatha meditation is very good. The Ngöndro type is also good. Vajrasattva practice is also good. It does not mean you always have to do the same thing and cannot change it. You can change what you do. You can do just Refuge sometimes. You can do Vajrasattva sometimes; or sometimes you can do Mandala Offering or Guru Yoga or Chenrezig. You can do Tonglen, mind-training, practice. Or you can just do sitting meditation. You can change, because all of them come to the same thing in the end. You can do Mahamudra practice – they all come to the same thing actually.

So, of these things, you can do whatever you understand and can connect with. And then sometimes you can have a break, and do something else. Sometimes, if you are always doing the same thing, you get a little bit bored by it, and then your inspiration is lost. Then, when you do something new for a certain number of days, you are re-inspired. Sometimes it is good to have a beginning, a middle and an end; like if you are doing one hundred thousand of something. Maybe nothing happens immediately that you complete one hundred thousand repetitions, but you have some sense of purpose to keep you going. It stops you getting too vague about what you are doing, or losing enthusiasm. So, sometimes it is good to have a little bit of that kind of a focus.

All this is really, however, the training *for* practice. All these formal practices and retreats, and so forth, I see as a training for practice. The real practice is your life: how you actually use these methods or ways of thinking or ways of being or ways of reacting, in your own, usual life. When you are working, when you are with people, when you have problems, when you have challenges, when negative emotions come: that is your practice. Your practice is your life. How you deal with your life, and how you face your problems, are the real path of practice.

The practice is not *Buddhist* practice. It is not about 'how to be a Buddhist.' Practice is about how to deal with your problems, how to be a better human being. The test is how you work there. If you feel you cannot practice, because you have too many troubles, then that is not practice. If you cannot practice, because you are having too good a time, then that is not practice. What is practice for, in that case? This, I think, is very important.

A Short Teaching on the Bardos

The Bardo is a concept, which is common to all Buddhist traditions. What we usually call the Bardo Teachings, for example The Six Bardos or The Four Bardos, come from teachings that are associated with the Vajrasattva practice. So it is not out of context that we have a few words on this here. It is a big subject so I am not saying everything about it here, of course.

The word *bardo* is a Tibetan word, which means 'in between' - 'hanging in between.' It can also be translated as 'transitory', 'in transit' or 'transient.' Sometimes people understand the Bardo to mean only the experience after death but it is not just that. From the point of view of the Four Bardo teachings or the Six Bardo teachings, every situation and every moment and every experience is a bardo experience, because it is a transient experience. It is something transitory. It is between things; it travels; it does not stay put. So, therefore, the whole cycles of life and death are all described as bardos. The whole cycle is included in the Four Bardos, or sometimes in Six Bardos.

When we talk about the Four Bardos, the first bardo is the Bardo of Life. That is now - from birth until death. This is called the Bardo of Life. Right from birth up until death, things are always changing. Things are always moving and always transitory. There is no certainty. There is no stopping; it is always moving forward.

There was once an advertisement I saw. It started by showing a woman in labour, about to give birth. Then there was a baby shooting out of her and then on out of the window and all the time crying, 'Aaaahhhh!' The baby was changing in mid-air as it moved; growing older and getting bigger and bigger until it was a young man; then becoming an old man, slowly, slowly, with teeth falling and hair falling; and then going direct to the grave. 'Aaaahhhh!' In one long jump. It may not be a very nice picture, not a pleasant one, but that is kind of the situation. It is the reality. The moment we are born we are heading towards death – maybe with a long, continuous cry!

This is an important part of the Bardo teachings: that there is nothing stopping, nothing holding still, nothing going back. It is a whole process of changing and going on to the next place - from birth heading to death and, in between, encountering all the problems and sufferings of samsara. That is life; that is the story.

But that is not the whole story. Life is not without opportunities. This is the main thing to understand from the Bardo teachings. If the reality was only problems and suffering and no other opportunity, then there would be nothing to talk about. But it is not like that. There are many opportunities. Every moment is seen as an opportunity to free oneself from the bondage of samsara.

Samsara is a state of habitual tendency, a state of mind, of reacting with ignorance and aversion and attachment. We have continuous pain and problems for this reason. But there is also, always, continuous opportunity to get out of this situation, to become free of this state of mind. Every moment allows us the possibility to understand that it is not necessary to have all these sufferings and pain and problems. At any moment, at any stage of the transition, there is this opportunity: not only during our lifetime, but also at the time of death, and also after death, and also at the time of rebirth. At any time of transition, there is always the chance and possibility to free ourselves from this bondage.

Therefore, we need to be aware. We do not need to remain trapped in this situation we are in. If we are talking about during our lifetime, we need to know how to not be totally entrapped in our situation. We need to learn how to lessen our attachment and aversion, our trying to run away and our trying to get. If we are trapped, it is possible that we can free ourselves from that. We need to allow ourselves to be self-liberated.

That is the reason we need to tame our mind. It is why we need to purify our mind. It is why we have to transcend our samsaric way of reacting. It is why we need to understand and experience the true nature of ourselves and the true nature of phenomena, of everything. If we can truly experience that, then there is nothing that is actually binding us. What is binding us is our own misunderstandings, our own habitual tendencies; our own way of seeing and our own negative emotions; our own experience and nothing else. That is why, from the Buddhist point of view, our problems are something that we create.

This means we can also free ourselves of our problems. There is always a possibility and a chance of this, and it is very important to work on this, not only for my own benefit but also for the benefit of every being. All our suffering comes out of this basic situation of misunderstanding: through birth, through death, through sickness, through old age; through getting what we don't want and not getting what we do want; all sorts of anguish, all sorts of mental and physical problems and tensions. So, it is necessary to focus ourselves and to make it our most cherished goal to work on our own liberation and the liberation of others. We need to find how to do that and then work on that.

We also need to do it now, because now is a very good opportunity. We have a precious human life, in which we can much more easily understand than many other life forms can. We have a much greater power of perception, power of understanding, power of changing things, power of transformation and innovation. We can look after ourselves and do things. We have use of language. We have a very big brain. Sometimes that works against us, also, but generally it is a good thing for us. So, therefore, when this opportunity is here we have to use it to work towards liberation. Dharma practice is exactly that.

The first part is to learn *how* to work on this. Everyone who is suffering, who has problems and pain, it is not because they *want* to have these. And it is not because they have not made any efforts not to have these. Everybody makes the utmost effort to be free from pain and suffering and problems. So why are we still having pain and problems and suffering? It is because we don't know how not to. So knowing how not to suffer is the most important thing. That is where the Buddha's teachings come in: all the experience and guidance of great masters is coming from here.

It is not enough, though, to have the knowledge of how to do something. Even if we know how to do things, if we don't *do* them then they will not happen. So that is why practice is important. Buddha said, 'My inheritance that I leave for the beings of the future is the teachings and the experiences.' The teachings are how to do things, the explanation of the way or the path. And the experiences are the actual experience of it; the liberation itself, the experience of enlightenment. Therefore, Buddha said, 'To really use my legacy, my lineage, is to study and practice.'

So, we need to learn how to do it and then we need to use it on ourselves and practise it. We cannot experience it unless we actually exercise it and use it in our daily life. That is not just about making a specific time for practice. That is important, to make time to learn and receive teachings; to make time for certain retreats and courses and things like that. That is also important. But the true practice is to really integrate these understandings into our life: How we look at things, how we see. How we react and how we 'be.' Only if we can do this, is there the possibility that we can liberate ourselves, that we can transform ourselves.

It is not that 'this is the Buddhist way' and I act like this in a shrine room and then not when I am not there. It is not that I need to become like another culture, like a Tibetan, that I need to dress like a Tibetan or something like that. It is not about bringing something else into my life. It is about living my own life in a way that is good for me, with compassion, with understanding, with wisdom; in a way that I can experience much more peace, much more tranquillity, much more kindness and joy, much less negativity. That is the practice.

The idea is not that I try to bring some other culture into my life, or I try to become something different from what I have been or the way people do things normally around me. When we talk about integrating the practice of Dharma into our lives we do not mean that kind of thing. It is not that kind of integration. Integration of Dharma is that we learn how to live in a way with less negativity, less tension, less aggression, less problematic, disturbed situations; and that we really start to do that. It is not about cultures or certain traditions of a particular way of life. It is about how I see and how I experience. Because of this, the most important bardo is actually the Bardo of Life.

The Bardo of Life is very transitory, very uncertain. Sometimes we feel it is very long but it is not so long. Sometimes it goes in the blink of an eye. The years can pass just like that, no? There is no certainty. We can't even say for sure if we will be here next year. This means it is now that we have to start to work. When we say we have to start to practise Dharma, it is not that we have to start to do something totally different. We don't have to stop doing everything we have already been doing - stop our job, stop our family or go somewhere else. It is not about that. It is within ourselves. It is about how to react; how to be a little bit mindful of how we are acting and reacting. And how I experience myself. It is just that.

In a way, to practise Dharma is very difficult because it is transforming our habitual tendencies. But in another way, it is not so difficult, because it is just about being a little bit aware of how we are acting and reacting and then choosing the best way for myself and for others. That is what

I want to do anyway! So I just remind myself of that as much as I can - in my day, maybe each hour, starting from now. That is the practice of Dharma. When we understand this, then it is a simple thing. It is not something too difficult to understand. It does not need too much knowledge or scholarship or intellectualising. Of course there are many things to learn, but it is not necessary to have a lot of knowledge before we can start. As I said before, our problem is to do with *not knowing*. That is the problem. So, the more we understand things clearly, the better it is. But this does not mean you have to be a great scholar. What we understand, we use that.

This is very important to remember because, otherwise, when we study Dharma, we can easily get lost in complications. Dharma, especially Tibetan Buddhism, is quite complicated because it comes from the tradition of the Indian universities. Tibetan Buddhism is based on the way Buddhism was taught in Nalanda University, in Vikramashila University, and other Indian universities at that time. That is the main part of what Tibet inherited. Most of the great masters that came to Tibet were the professors from these universities, including Khenpo Bodhisattva (Shantarakshita), Kamalashila, Vimalamitra, Padmasambhava, Naropa and many others. All of these great masters were professors from the Indian universities. And what they brought to Tibet were the complete Sutras and Tantras - the Sravakayana, Bodhisattvayana and Vajrayana; the complete state of the teachings. This includes many treatises, many details, many debates and so on. It is vast. You can spend your whole life studying them and still only know a little bit. It is very, very vast. But it is not necessary that one should know everything.

The important thing is to know what is most essential, and to understand what it is that we can practise - and then to practise what you understand. Sometimes we study something and, when we hear a nice instruction which is very clear and understandable and we agree with it, we think, 'Oh, that's nice. I understand that. No problem.' And we mentally put it over on one side. Then something comes which may not be very easy to understand. It is not very clear, a little bit complicated and kind of profound. We think, 'Oh, I don't understand that very much.' And mentally we put it over to another side. But then we find that, as we go along, there is nothing in front of us that we are actively working with. That is not the way. Maybe it is helpful to keep some things we don't understand over to one side, so we can look at them at a later time. But it is very important to keep the things we do understand close by, in the forefront of our mind, and really use them in our life. If we can do that, that may be enough. This is the attitude for the Bardo of Life.

The Bardo of Life is very important because what we understand and what we do now all make imprints on us. And the imprints we make now all affect our consequent transition. How we can be at the time of death, how we can react at that time, is very much affected by what we know, and how we practise, now. We cannot suddenly change our way of reacting and being. It is very difficult. It is not totally impossible but it is very difficult. That is why people sometimes say that the whole practice of life is like a preparation for death. Many Tibetans see it like this: the practices done during life are seen as a preparation for death and for later lives.

This is what we talk about whenever we consider karma. Karma is not necessarily a thing that you do and you get a certain result. It is not about every action bringing a certain punishment or reward. Every action - especially strong actions or reactions fuelled by strong emotions - makes an impression on my psyche or on my personality. That is why it affects the way I generally react. If I am acting and reacting in a negative way all my life, it would be very difficult to suddenly act in a positive way at the time of death, and afterwards. If I have been acting and reacting in a positive way, more or less, in life, then it becomes easier to react like that at the time of death and afterwards. That is why our practice now is very important, even if we only do a little bit. Most important is how we react to things: how upset we get; how much we become shocked; how much we are traumatised; how much we react to intense emotions with negativity. Whenever we notice we are starting to do these things and go down this path, we have to change how we are behaving. We have to tell ourselves, 'This is not the way.' We have to work on our reactions. This understanding and this practice will also affect our death.

The Bardo of Death is from the time we start to degenerate and our body starts to die, up until the time our mind is 'kind of dead.' Our body starts to die when the five elements of the body start to disintegrate. This is the starting point of death. There is a process, which you can read about in the Teachings of the Bardo if you want to, including how the experience would be. When all the five elements – the Fire element, Earth element, Water element, Air element and Space element – are in balance, then we are living and well. When they become imbalanced, then we get sick. For example, if some of the elements become too active or strong and some of the elements become too weak or under-expressed, then we get sick. When the balance is totally disrupted, then we die. This is how it is for me, for you, for a flower, for the world, for anything. When everything is in balance, then it is living and thriving. When it is a little out of balance, then it is deteriorating. And when it is disrupted, it is falling apart, it is dying.

In the same way, the body dies. Our body is changing all the time but it is usually changing within a degree of balance. When death comes, it is not only changing but changing totally out of balance and therefore it is falling apart. When our body dies, then our mind also ceases to be as it has been. The body and mind have a very strong link. They are totally interdependent. The mind is totally dependent on the body. The body is totally dependent on the mind. That is how we are living. So, therefore, when we die, not only the body disintegrates but also the mind.

The way we have all these thoughts and emotions, the way our brain works, also disappears. All our gross emotions and gross intelligences, all fall away. There is a stage at which all these mental factors dissolve. When the mental factors dissolve, our mind goes into our most subtle and most basic state of being. That is what we call death. Grossly speaking, the mind 'goes off,' the body disintegrates, we stop breathing and then our brain stops working. And, we could say, our mind stops working. It goes to the deepest level of consciousness or unconsciousness. All the steps leading to this make up the Bardo of Death.

There are also many opportunities in the Bardo of Death, from the Buddhist way of understanding. The Bardo of Death offers many opportunities for us to become transformed or self-liberated. This is because it is a very strong experience. When these things are happening and we are disintegrating in our body and mind, we have the chance to really allow ourselves to let go. We are always used to reacting with aversion and attachment: wanting and not wanting; fighting against things and running after things. We try to hold on to life. We are very afraid of dying. The stronger that way of reacting is, the more painful it is for us to die. But it does not stop us from dying. When our time comes, there is nothing we can do to stop ourselves dying. But we can understand it is a process, like any other process. There is no need to be afraid of dying. There is no need to hold on to life. There is no need because there is nothing you can do about it; it is a process.

It is a process of going deeper into our consciousness. We do not become totally extinct. We just go from gross experience to the subtlest experience. So, if we can really learn how to remain and at the same time allow ourselves to let go, there is a great opportunity here. Meditation is to help this – to learn how to experience our most natural and original state of experience. The state where thoughts do not happen and emotions do not happen; but there is awareness, subtle awareness, which is not like linear consciousness, but is just being, completely just being. Maybe we could say it is not a left-brain kind of a consciousness but a right-brain kind of consciousness. There is no separation. There is no identification. There is no duality. That is the kind of experience we are talking about here.

When we know this is the way it is, there is no reason for us to struggle against our experience. There is nothing to get rid of. There is nothing to gain. But we need to understand this deeply and experientially. It does not work just to understand it in theory. That is why we have to practise meditation now. When we can understand this deeply and experientially, then death is not a death. Death is a liberation. Death becomes enlightenment. Death becomes self-liberation. Death becomes going into your natural state of being – the most wonderful thing to happen. There is nothing negative about it. Those who are really good at this, go into Samadhi at the time of death. For them, it is not a death, it is a meditation. Even if we can't do that but we can allow ourselves to rest without feeling stressed, without problem, then, depending on how experienced we are, there is a big chance of liberation at this stage.

If we can really recognise this at this stage, and be aware of the most subtle awareness, then that is enlightenment. We experience the clear light. Sometimes they say it is like the child recognising the mother. When a child sees their mother, they are very happy. They are not afraid. They just go, in total confidence and trust, into the mother's lap and fall asleep. In the same way, if you are truly able to do like that, then you experience enlightenment. You experience the Buddha's experience: wisdom and compassion and selflessness. Clear light, Mahamudra and Dzogchen, all these things we discuss, you actually experience them. That is what it is all about: that is the way you are.

When you can experience the way you truly are then you are liberated, then and there. So death is regarded as very important because it is the strongest experience we will have. It is a very great opportunity to get this experiential understanding of enlightenment. If you miss that chance, if you cannot manage to be deeply quiet and relaxed; if you are too afraid and you do not recognise your nature at that time, then it is just like falling asleep or fainting - going into darkness.

But it does not remain like that; that is the understanding and the experience. It is the nature of the mind that it manifests again and again. Therefore, it starts to manifest again. That is when the Bardo of Dharmata comes, the third bardo. When we wake up from that most subtlest state of our consciousness, first we have different kinds of experiences, of sounds, lights and so on. There are experiences of forms, powerful experiences of strong lights, strong sounds, mild sounds and lights, all sorts of forms coming out. There is also a very strong opportunity for liberation here.

So far, through our life, everything we experience as happening, we experience as happening 'to me.' If there is sound or light it is 'out there.' Everything is 'out there' and I feel it is happening 'to me.' However, every experience I have happens within my experience. There is no experience that can happen outside the sphere of my mind. Every experience I have is within my mind. So everything *is* my mind, in a way. But, because we have this way of experiencing and reacting - 'This is happening to me... it should not be like this...it is so bad because it is happening to me...he is doing this...she is doing that....it is not good for me...' - we see it all as an outward thing, that we are the victim of what happens to us. We do not realise that all our experiences are our own experience. It is me; it is happening within me; it is a radiance of my own experience. There is nothing that is not within the radiance of my own experience.

We need to start to learn this now. When we understand it a little bit more deeply, then at the time of the Bardo of Dharmata, we have an opportunity to see more clearly that all our experience is completely our own. Because we are dead. There is nothing else there. We might experience strong lights and sounds and forms; they might be wrathful or ugly or unpleasant or pleasant or beautiful. But whatever experience we have, if we can recognise it is not 'out there' but it is our own experience; when we see that, then there is nothing to run away from;

there is nothing to run after. When we know that, then everything is perfect; everything is enlightened; everything is Buddha; everything is a mandala.

If you don't see it like that, but you see it as something very bad, something very difficult, everything as problematic, then it is samsara. That is why we start to practise now, that everything is Vajrasattva, or similarly. Whatever practice we do - Vajrasattva, Mandala Offering, Peaceful and Wrathful Deities and all different deities - they are all for that. To see that ultimately anything, everything, nice things, difficult things, anything that you see, is okay. Everything is emptiness and appearance. So, therefore, there is nothing wrong; it is perfect; it is mandala. It is okay; it is your own experience. So, therefore, it is a deity: there is nothing negative, nothing wrong.

When we start to experience like that, then, yes, everything that we experience is perfect, is a mandala. And we become enlightened in that. So the Bardo of Dharmata is regarded as a very important experience where you can also become completely liberated and enlightened. You can become one with everything you have been hearing about in Dharma study. Of course, these experiences could also be very traumatic. But when you understand it is all your own experience, it is all the radiance of your own mind, there is nothing other than that; then you don't have to react with aversion. There is nothing shocking. You can't find it traumatic if it is just something you created yourself. When we know it is just our own mind, we can't be traumatised by it. Instead, we can be liberated: we know everything is okay.

This is another opportunity. If we recognise it and can liberate ourselves at that time, then the next stage does not have to come. Instead, we are free by ourselves. So we can generate whatever we want. But if we don't become liberated, because of our ignorance, because of too much fear and aversion and things like that, then we come into the fourth bardo: the Bardo of Becoming.

We may not even realise that we are dead up until then - but we are! All our experience of the past comes back and we might start wondering, 'What's wrong with me? - Nobody is talking to me; nobody even smiles at me...' Then we see our body there, dead. Till then, we might be doubtful about whether we are dead or not. Sometimes this is what we call 'bardo,' just this experience. Then, when we realise we are dead, we might get angry, or we might feel sad. If you continue to have the same way of reacting as you have now, you will look at people and how they are doing things and you may become even more upset, for instance, if they are fighting over your possessions. But if you become too upset, too negative or too angry, that is very bad for you. Because you are only mind at that time. There is always a feeling of a body but at this stage it is only a bardo body, like a body of light. You could pass through a wall, for example.

If you then realise you are dead, you realise you don't have to worry about your possessions anymore; you don't have to be angry or upset. You just have to concentrate on something positive. This is where you can, again, gain much benefit if you stop reacting to things that are going on with so much attachment or aversion. You can say, instead, 'Okay, this is the time I must really put my mind in order. The people I am attached to, my family, I cannot do anything for them anymore anyway. I just have to leave them to take care of themselves. If they can't manage it, that is their problem.' There is nothing you can do – you are dead. 'They will dispose of my body. Whether they will burn it or bury it or throw it into the bin, I cannot influence it now. It is up to them. So, I just concentrate on something positive.'

If you visualise Vajrasattva, then you become Vajrasattva, because you are only mind at that time. Whatever you visualise, that *is* you. Wherever you want to go, you are there. You don't need to take an aeroplane; you just go, instantaneously. Because you have no body, wherever you think of, you are there. If you want to go to Dewachen, then you are in

Dewachen. If, at that time, you can concentrate on something positive, something enlightened, something good, then you become that.

That is why it is very important to train ourselves to focus our mind on something positive. It is good to relax and make your mind calm, but we also need to train to be positive. We need to see ourselves as an enlightened being and concentrate on that. So, there is a very strong possibility to be liberated and become enlightened also at this stage. But if you cannot manage that, the cycle begins again. The bardo teachings are all about this. There are countless opportunities: If you cannot do this, then try that. If you cannot do that, then try the next thing. And so on. If you cannot manage to become free at this stage, then you will be reborn.

Children's experience of dying

Student: Do you think it is easier for very young children, if they have to go through this process? I can remember when I was a young child, about four years old, and I had very bad meningitis. I can remember people around me praying, but I didn't have any fear. I didn't know what was happening but I had an experience like what you were describing: I saw coloured lights and heard angels singing. So I wondered, if children haven't got the baggage we have later in life, if it is easier for them to go with the experience as it happens? Depending on the type of death of course. But they haven't got all the mental constructs and so on that we have as adults – does that make it easier?

Rinpoche: Children have less experience of this life, so, therefore, they are more innocent. They have fewer concepts. But children also have fear; they have anger; they have things they like and things they don't like. They experience 'pain' and 'no pain,' 'happiness' and 'not happiness.' I don't see children as being like a clean slate. I can see this clearly because I have so many nieces and nephews. I am the oldest of six brothers and sisters and I now have ten nieces and nephews. Just among them, I see that a child has a very clear and definite, strong personality and it is there from the day they are born. And they are so different from each other.

So I am sure that children are not like a clean slate. Of course they are innocent and they trust grown-ups. But even little children don't want to suffer. They don't want to be hungry. They don't want to be in pain. They want to be loved. We can see their emotions. And then each child has its own personality. Some are more angry; some are less angry - all sorts of things. All these factors will be there even if a child has to go through death.

Putting animals to sleep

Student: If an animal is very old and suffering very much in its body, what would be your view on putting that animal to sleep, out of compassion?

Rinpoche: This is a very common question. I think it depends on what you think is the right thing to do. If an animal is really suffering and in a lot of pain, I think maybe we don't need to let it continue to suffer. This question is also asked over human beings, whether it should be allowed to assist someone to die.

From the Buddhist point of view it is seen like this: We have the practice of *phowa* [transference of consciousness at death] and it is said, if you are really good at this practice, you can transfer your consciousness and thus die. But it is said that, even if you can do that, you should not do it, even if you are in pain or something like that, unless you are one hundred percent sure you are dying. You should do everything you can to cure or heal yourself, to prevent yourself from dying. Only then, when you have done everything you can, if you are still one hundred percent sure you are dying, then it is okay to do *phowa* on yourself and die. Otherwise, you should not.

This is the general understanding from the Buddhist point of view: If you are putting an end to a life, it is not a good thing to do. But if there is too much suffering and the death is imminent very soon, then it is okay. Making a law is another thing. I see a difference here - because then people could misuse that law. I have sometimes seen people 'waiting' for someone to die. Sometimes people find it very hard to die. Even when they are old and very sick and it is clear they will die very soon, they still find it hard to die. A large proportion of medical expenditure on someone may even come at this stage. But still you cannot help someone to die more quickly. Whereas with animals, many people help animals to die and I think that if they are in a lot of pain, then it is understandable. Then, I think it is not too bad to do that.

Rebirth

How my next life will be does not depend on someone else 'making an order' and then that is how I will be. It depends on how I am and how I react. It is just a continuation of how I have already been. So, if I continue to react with anger and negativity, disturbed, with lots of tension, then I will become like that: I will take a negative rebirth. But if I react in a positive way, my rebirth becomes more positive. What kind of rebirth I get is not 'ordered' by somebody. It is a continuation of how I react and how I am.

If you can act with compassion, with kindness, with joy, with peace, then naturally your rebirth can be something positive and something beneficial. There are lots of different instructions on how to eliminate negative rebirths. But I don't think you need to hear all these - because you will already have become enlightened before that stage!

Somehow, then, you get conceived. We have this predisposition that we are always running away from something and running towards something else. If we continue to do that, therefore, we will be running away and when we find something we feel is good we will try to stay there and hold on to that. That is how we get reborn, how we get conceived. As long as we are in the samsaric state of mind we go on like that. We go on in this cycle, without freedom - that is the samsaric aspect. Then, when we realise we do not have to have fear and negative reactions, it is not that we discontinue. There is nothing to discontinue. But we become free. If we want to we can take rebirth, but we do not have to. What rebirth we take, or when or where, is up to us.

When you are liberated it means you do not have to think about your own welfare too much, because you know that you will always be okay. That is the key. If you know that, whatever happens, you will always be okay, then you do not have to be afraid of anything. You do not have to run away from anything, or after anything. You have no aversion and no attachment. But you still have love and compassion. You can see what needs to be done. You can see the problems of others and see how they do not realise what is going on. So then you work as a Bodhisattva. And become a greater and greater Bodhisattva.

'*Yourself* [3]

Mischief is yours.
Sorrow is yours.
But virtue also is yours,
And purity.

You are the source
Of all purity and all impurity.

No one purifies another.'

Root Text

Brief Recitations for the Four Preliminary Practices

By His Holiness the 17th Karmapa

Glorious, powerful, omnipresent Lord Vajradhara,

Principal of all Buddha families – Guru Karmapa;

Origin of all mandalas, glory of samsara and nirvana –
Yidam Vajrayogini;

Those who have power over enlightened activity –
dharma protectors Bernakchen and consort;

This yogi bows down to you with one-pointed respect –
please protect me forever with your noble compassion.

*Once individuals have purified their mindstreams with the
common preliminary practices, they should excellently request
empowerment and instruction from a qualified guru and then
train in the recitation meditation of Mahamudra's extraordinary
preliminary practices as follows:*

I. Going for Refuge and Giving Rise to Bodhichitta

First, so that everything you do will accord with the dharma, go for refuge and give rise to Bodhicitta in two ways: during meditation sessions and in between meditation sessions.

During meditation sessions, leave worldly concerns and other activities aside, sit in a proper meditation posture on a comfortable seat, and recite:

Before me in the sky is the Guru Vajradhara,
Surrounded by the gurus of the lineage of meaning and blessings
And gurus with whom I have dharmic connections of faith.
In front are the yidams, to the right are the Buddhas.
Behind is the sacred dharma; to the left, the sangha.
All are surrounded by ocean-like retinues of their own kind.
My mothers, sentient beings, and I stand together
As the sources of refuge gaze down upon us.
One-pointedly, we go for refuge and arouse bodhichitta.

All sentient beings and I go for refuge to the gurus.
We go for refuge to the yidams.
We go for refuge to the buddhas.
We go for refuge to the dharma.
We go for refuge to the sangha.

Go to these five jewels for refuge as many times as possible.

Until I reach enlightenment's essence,
I go for refuge to the buddhas.
To the dharma and the assembly
Of bodhisattvas, too, I go for refuge.
Just as the sugatas of the past
Aroused the mind of bodhichitta;
Just as they followed step-by-step
The training of the bodhisattvas,
So, too, shall I, to benefit wanderers
Arouse the mind of bodhichitta.
So, too, shall I follow step-by-step,
The bodhisattva's training.

Recite three times.

Then recite the following:

May precious and supreme bodhichitta
Arise where it has not arisen,
Not diminish where it has arisen,
And continually increase and increase.

Finally, the sources of refuge melt into light and then become one with me.

Second, between sessions, do not be indifferent. Take up the antidotes: Strive to increase devotion to the guru, to develop as much faith in the rare and supreme jewels as possible, and to have greater and greater compassion for sentient beings.

II. Vajrasattva Meditation and Recitation

The Vajrasattva meditation and recitation practice, which purifies negativity and obscurations, has two parts. First, during meditation sessions, recite:

Above the crown of my head, on a lotus-moon seat,
Is Guru Vajrasattva, white in colour, adorned with ornaments,
With one face and two arms,
Holding a vajra with his right hand and a bell with his left, and
seated in vajra posture.

Clearly visualise at Vajrasattva's heart centre a moon disc, upon which sits a HUM, encircled by the mantra garland. Due to your supplicating him, a stream of amrita fills his body and descends from his right big toe, entering the Brahma aperture at the top of your head. All your obscurations and past negative actions, embodied in a substance that looks like ink or dark smoke, leave your body as all of your body's parts are filled with amrita. While doing this visualisation, recite Vajrasattva's mantra as many times as you can:

OM VAJRASATTVA SAMAYAM ANUPALAYA
VAJRASATTVA TVENOPATISHTHA DRIDHO ME
BHAVA SUTOSHYO ME BHAVA SUPOSHYO ME
BHAVA ANURAKTO ME BHAVA SARVA-SIDDHIM
ME PRAYACCHA SARVA-KARMASU CHA ME
CHITTAM SHREYAH KURU HUM HA HA HA HA
HOH BHAGAVAN SARVA-TATHAGATA VAJRA MA ME
MUNCHA VAJRI BHAVA MAHASAMAYASATTVA AH

OM VAJRASATTVA HUM [4]

ༀ་བཛྲ་ས་ཏྭ་ས་མ་ཡ། མ་ནུ་པཱ་ལ་ཡ།

བཛྲ་ས་ཏྭ་ཏེ་ནོ་པ་ཏིཥྛ་དྲྀ་ཌྷོ་མེ་བྷ་ཝ།

སུ་ཏོ་ཥྱོ་མེ་བྷ་ཝ། སུ་པོ་ཥྱོ་མེ་བྷ་ཝ།

ཨ་ནུ་རཀྟོ་མེ་བྷ་ཝ། སརྦ་སིདྡྷིམྨེ་པྲ་ཡ་ཙྪ།

སརྦ་ཀརྨ་སུ་ཙ་མེ། ཙིཏྟཾ་ཤྲི་ཡཿཀུ་རུ་ཧཱུྂ།

ཧ་ཧ་ཧ་ཧ་ཧོཿ བྷ་ག་ཝན།

སརྦ་ཏ་ཐཱ་ག་ཏ་བཛྲ་མཱ་མེ་མུཉྩ།

བཛྲཱི་བྷ་ཝ་མ་ཧཱ་ས་མ་ཡ་ས་ཏྭ་ཨཱཿ

*Then, confess your past negative actions and vow not to perform them
again by reciting the following:*

Noble ones who know and see everything, think of us.

Since beginningless time,

Under the power of the three poisons,

We have transgressed the three vows and the victors' commands

In body, speech and mind.

We admit and confess these downfalls and misdeeds

And promise not to do them again – may we not experience

their results.

*Saying this, confess and resolve not to repeat your misdeeds.
Vajrasattva says, "Your misdeeds are purified," and is pleased. He
melts into light and dissolves into you.*

Rest in equipoise.

*Second, between sessions: whatever afflictions or thoughts arise,
be mindful of them as soon as they arise. Completely cut through
them and rest in freedom from fixation. Whatever sentient beings
you see, hear or think of – especially those who have done terrible
misdeeds – visualise Vajrasattva above their heads and recite the
hundred-syllable mantra.*

*As it was needed quickly, the one called Karmapa, Ogyen Trinley, composed
this according to the fifth Shamar's pith instructions on the preliminaries
on the 9th day of the waxing phase of the 6th Tibetan month at the temple of
Gyuto, 3rd August 2006.*

*[Note: not included here are parts III and IV of the Preliminary Practices:
The Mandala Offering and Guru Yoga practices.]*

ཨོཾ་བཛྲ་མ་ར་ཏུ་ཧཱུྃ།

Dedication

All my babbling,
In the name of Dharma
Has been set down faithfully
By my dear students of pure vision.

I pray that at least a fraction of the wisdom
Of those enlightened teachers
Who tirelessly trained me
Shines through this mass of incoherence.

May the sincere efforts of all those
Who have worked tirelessly
Result in spreading the true meaning of Dharma
To all who are inspired to know.

May this help dispel the darkness of ignorance
In the minds of all living beings
And lead them to complete realisation
Free from all fear.

Ringu Tulku

Glossary and Notes

Editor's Note: Wherever possible the descriptions in the glossaries of the Heart Wisdom books include Ringu Tulku's own words, gathered from a variety of teaching sources. But, as this is not always possible, the glossary is offered as a help to the reader and not a definitive authority.

Abhidharma (Sanskrit; *ngön pa dzö* Tibetan) is an authoritative scripture on Buddhist metaphysics according to the Sravakayana or Foundational Vehicle. Otherwise known as 'The Compendium of Abhidharma' or 'The Treasure House of Knowledge,' it was written by Vasubandhu (*circa* 4th century CE), and concerns the difference between the phenomena of *samsara* and *nirvana* (see below).

Amrita (Sanskrit; *dütsi* Tibetan) literally means the immortal; the nectar (*tsi*) that conquers the demon (*dü*) of death; symbol of wisdom.

Arhat (Sanskrit; *dracompa* Tibetan) literally means 'foe destroyer;' one who has overcome the enemies of conflicting emotions and has realised the non-existence of a personal self; the goal of the Sravakayana or fundamental vehicle.

Atisha (982 – 1054) (Sanskrit; *Jowo Atisha* Tibetan), also known as Dipamkara, was a great Indian master and scholar, and one of the main teachers at the monastic university of Vikramashila. He spent the last ten years of his life teaching in Tibet, where his followers founded the Kadampa school. His most celebrated text is the *Lamp for the Path to Enlightenment,* which he wrote for the Tibetan people and which became the source for the *Lamrim,* or graduated path, tradition, found in all schools of Tibetan Buddhism.

Attachment is holding on too strongly to something, clinging to it: you get too close to something you perceive as nice, so that your relating with it takes on a 'sticky' kind of feeling.

Avalokiteshvara (Sanskrit) see *Chenrezig.*

Aversion is a mind quality of rejecting or pushing something away; wishing it were not there and trying to eliminate it or get away from it.

Bardo (Tibetan) literally means 'in between.' It can also be translated as 'in transit' or 'transient.' Sometimes the term Bardo is reserved for the experience after death, before the next rebirth, but the term can also mean any time. Every situation and every moment and every experience is a bardo experience, because it is a transient experience. It is something transitory, between things; it does not stay put. The whole cycle of life and death are all described as bardos, sometimes as the Four Bardos or the Six Bardos. The Four Bardos are the Bardo of Life; the Bardo of Death; the Bardo of Dharmata; the Bardo of Becoming.

Bodhicitta (also spelled *Bodhichitta* Sanskrit; *changchub kyi sem* Tibetan) is the heart essence of the Buddha, of enlightenment. The root of the word, *Bodh*, means 'to know, to have the full understanding' and *citta* refers to the heart-mind or 'heart feeling'. In a practical sense, Bodhicitta is compassion imbued with wisdom.

Bodhisattva (Sanskrit; *changchub sempa* Tibetan) comes from the root *bodh* which means to know, to have the full understanding. The term describes a being who has made a commitment to work for the benefit of others to bring them to a state of lasting peace and happiness and freedom from all suffering. A Bodhisattva does not have to be a Buddhist but can come from any spiritual tradition or none. The key thing is that they have this compassionate wish to free all beings from suffering, informed by the wisdom of knowing this freedom is possible.

Buddha nature or **Buddhanature** (*Sugatagarba* Sanskrit; *desheg nyingpo* Tibetan) refers to the fundamental, true nature of all beings, free from all obscurations and distortions. Ultimately, our true nature and the true nature of all beings is inseparable from the nature of Buddha. It is the 'primordial goodness' of sentient beings, an innate all-pervasive primordial purity.

Buddha Shakyamuni, the historical Buddha, was born a Prince in North East India about 500 B.C.E. and left home to discover the causes of suffering. He gave the teachings that have come down the centuries to be called Buddhism.

Chenrezig (Tibetan; *Avalokiteshvara* Sanskrit) is the embodiment of the compassionate aspect of the mind of the Buddhas. He is revered as the patron deity of Tibet, his most common forms being the Four-armed and the Thousand-armed Chenrezig. The four arms represent the Four Immeasurables and the thousand arms represent unlimited compassionate activity throughout space and time, each hand having an eye in its palm. [Although Chenrezig is represented in male form in Tibet, Avalokiteshvara is translated as Kuan Yin in the Chinese tradition and as Kwannon in the Japanese, both represented in female form.] The mantra of Chenrezig is one of the best known: *OM MANI PEME HUNG*.

Clear Light *(ösal* Tibetan) or Luminous *(ö)* Clarity *(sal)* is the true nature of our mind, generally hidden under obscuration but nevertheless its true state, and so possible to experience when all obscuration is cleared away.

Dakini see *Khandro.*

Deity / Deities (*istadevata* Sanskrit; *yidam* Tibetan) in Buddhism, are representations of the embodiment of enlightened mind. They are visualised or depicted in various forms to bring out different aspects of its essential purity. During formal practice a deity may be visualised in front of or above the practitioner or as the practitioner him or herself. Deities encourage us to see the pure state of reality, by which we mean the state that does not bind us or create problems and is, therefore, a liberating state.

Dewachen (Tibetan; *Sukhavati* Sanskrit) is the 'Pureland' of Buddha Amitabha: a state of mind of ultimate peace and happiness.

Dharma (Sanskrit; *chö* Tibetan) The word dharma has many uses. In its widest sense it means all that can be known, or the way things are. The other main meaning is the teachings of the Buddha; also called the *Buddhadharma,* which refers to the entire body of oral and written Buddhist teachings, including the literal teachings and that which is learnt through practising them.

Dharmata (Sanskrit; *chönyi* Tibetan) is the ultimate nature or reality of things; synonymous with Emptiness. See *Emptiness.*

Dorje see *Vajra.*

Dorje Sempa is the Tibetan translation of Vajrasattva. *Dorje* has the same meaning as *vajra* (see *vajra*) and *Sempa* means 'hero' or 'brave one.'

Duhkha (Sanskrit; *Dukkha* Pali; *dugngal* Tibetan) means discontent, or suffering; the basic unsatisfactory nature of how we experience life. Taught by the Buddha, in his foundational teaching of The Four Noble Truths, to be a hallmark of life. The Four Noble Truths also teach the causes and conditions that give rise to *duhkha* and the path to its cessation.

Dzogchen or **Dzogpa Chenpo** (Tibetan; *Ati Yoga* Sanskrit) literally translates as 'Great Completion' or 'Great Perfection.' It is a body of teachings and practices that are considered to be the highest of the Inner Tantra of the Nyingma School of Tibetan Buddhism, aimed at helping a practitioner to achieve primordial true nature, the natural state. The practice of Dzogchen ultimately brings the same result as Mahamudra.

Empowerment (*abhisheka* Sanskrit; *wang* Tibetan) is a ceremony conferring the blessing and transmission of the lineage. It also serves as a teaching and an introduction to a specific practice. It is a bit like a guided meditation, that a qualified master leads students through, together invoking the blessings of the lineage and making an authentic link to that practice. To be complete, the transmission of the text (*lung*) and the explanations / instructions (*tri*) must also be received. The Empowerment, Transmission and Instruction are often referred to as the '*Wang, Lung and Tri*' and are an indispensable door to tantric practices.

Emptiness (*shunyata* Sanskrit; *tong pa nyi* Tibetan) The Buddha taught in the second turning of the wheel of Dharma, that all phenomena have no real, independent existence of their own. They only appear to exist as separate, nameable entities because of the way we commonly, conceptually, see things. But in themselves, all things are 'empty' of inherent existence. This includes our 'self', which we habitually unconsciously mistake to be an independently-existing, separate phenomenon. Instead, everything exists in an interdependent way and this is what the term emptiness refers to. Ringu Tulku says in *Like Dreams and Clouds*: 'Emptiness does not mean there is nothing; emptiness means the way everything is, the way everything magically manifests.'

Five Buddha Families represent different aspects of transformation or enlightenment, and, together, the full mandala of enlightened mind. The five families are: the Vajra family, presided over by the Buddha Akshobhya; the Ratna (jewel) family, presided over by Ratnasambhava; the Padme (lotus) family, presided over by Amitabha; the Karma family, presided over by Amoghasiddhi; and the Buddha family, presided over by Vairochana. These five Buddhas have feminine counterparts, which represent the Five Elements: Mamaki represents the completely pure element of Water and is paired with Akshobhya; Buddhalochana represents the completely pure element of Earth and is paired with Ratnasambhava; Pandaravasini represents the completely pure element of Fire and is paired with Amitabha; Samayatara represents the completely pure element of Wind and is paired with Amoghasiddhi; Dhatvishvari represents the completely pure element of Space and is paired with Vairochana.

Guru Padmasambhava, also known as **Guru Pema** and **Guru Rinpoche,** in a historical sense, was an 8th century Indian Buddhist Master who was invited by King Trisong Detsen to re-establish Buddhism in Tibet, which included dealing with the negative influences hindering the work of Buddhist monks. Together with Shantarakshita, he supervised the translation of the Dharma into the Tibetan language. Padmasambhava left Tibet in 774 C.E. without having completed the full transmission of the *Dzogchen* path to enlightenment. Seeing that the times were not ripe, he buried further texts on Dzogchen (see *terma*) to be unearthed and studied in later times. The Nyingma School of Tibetan Buddhism recognises him as their root guru. Guru Rinpoche can also be seen as representing the archetypal or universal teacher, a perfect role model. In this sense, he is the guiding power, which emanates from pure mind anywhere in time and space, and a mirror of our own innate wisdom mind.

Guru Yoga (*lamay naljor* Tibetan) is the practice of devotion to the guru and, through receiving blessing, blending indivisibly with the mind of the guru.

Kamalashila (Sanskrit; *Pemay Ngangtsul* Tibetan) (740–795) was the main disciple of the great abbot Shantarakshita. He famously defeated a Chinese master in debate at Samye around 792 AD, with the result that the Tibetans followed the Indian philosophical tradition of Madhyamika rather than the Chinese school.

Karma (Sanskrit; *lay* Tibetan) literally means 'action.' It refers to the cycle of cause and effect that is set up through our actions. Actions coloured or motivated by *klesha* (see below), for example, anger or desire, will tend to create results in keeping with that action and also increase our tendency to do similar actions.

These tendencies become ingrained in us and become our habitual way of being, which is our karma. According to our level of awareness, we can change our karma through consciously refining our actions.

Khandro (Tibetan; *dakini* Sanskrit) has many different interpretations but one way of describing the meaning, especially of the aspect called the 'wisdom dakini' is to look at the translation into Tibetan: *Kha* means 'the sky' and *dro* means 'goer:' 'those who travel in the space.' This refers to those who 'go in the space of the natural sphere:' those people who can travel in the natural state, or in natural phenomena, through their own wisdom and power. It means one who understands the Dharma, one who has the experience of the Dharma. The Khandro is the one who holds the true essence of the Dharma.

Kleshas (Sanskrit; *nyön mong* Tibetan) are translated as mental defilements, mind poisons or negative emotions. They include any emotion or mind state that disturbs or distorts consciousness. They bring forth our experience of suffering and prevent our experience of love, joy and happiness. The three main kleshas are desire, anger and ignorance. Combinations of these give rise to the five kleshas, which are these three plus pride and envy / jealousy.

Lama (Tibetan; *guru* Sanskrit) means teacher or master. *La* refers to there being nobody higher in terms of spiritual accomplishment and *ma* refers to compassion like a mother. Thus both wisdom and compassion are brought to fruition together in the lama. The word has the connotation of 'heavy' or 'weighty,' indicating the guru or lama is heavy with positive attributes and kindness.

Lung (Tibetan) is the reading transmission of a practice, whereby a qualified master reads through the practice in the presence of students who receive, in that way, the *lung*.

Mahamudra (Sanskrit; *cha ja chen po* or *chak chen* Tibetan) literally means 'Great Seal' or 'Great Symbol,' referring to the way in which all phenomena are 'sealed' by their primordially perfect true nature. The term can denote the teaching, meditation practice or accomplishment of Mahamudra. The meditation consists in perceiving the mind directly rather than through rational analysis, and relies on a direct introduction to the nature of the essence of the mind. This form of meditation is traced back to Saraha (10th century), and was passed down in the Kagyu school through Marpa. The accomplishment lies in experiencing the non-duality of the phenomenal world and emptiness: perceiving how the two are not separate. This experience can also be called the union of emptiness and luminosity.

Mahayana (Sanskrit; *tek pa chen po* Tibetan) translates as 'Great Vehicle.' This is the second vehicle of Buddhism, and emphasises the teachings on Bodhicitta, compassion, and interdependence. It expands on the teachings of the Sravakayana (the foundational vehicle of Buddhism) and sees the purpose of enlightenment as being the liberation of *all* sentient beings from suffering, as well as oneself. This is the path of the Bodhisattva (see above) and so may also be called the Bodhisattvayana. See also *Sravakayana.*

Mala (Sanskrit; *trengwa* Tibetan) is a string of beads, usually one hundred and eight, used for counting mantra recitations. They can be made of many different materials; commonly sandalwood, or other woods, semi-precious stones or Bodhi seeds.

Mandala (Sanskrit; *kyil khor* Tibetan) meaning a circle, normally having a centre and an edge, it literally refers to everything that exists within the periphery of the circle. In Buddhism, the mandala of a teacher refers to everything and everyone associated with that person. Mandala can also refer to an actual or graphic representation that symbolises all aspects of a deity and acts as a support for meditation. It can also be a symbolic representation of the entire universe, which can be visualised and offered in its purest form for the benefit of all beings.

Mandala Offering (Sanskrit; *kyil khor* Tibetan) is an offering that is visualised as the entire universe. It traditionally comprises thirty-seven aspects and is often made as part of a request to receive Dharma teachings; one of the Four Extraordinary Foundational practices of the Ngöndro. See *Ngöndro.*

Manjushri is one of the eight main Bodhisattvas. He is the personification of the perfection of wisdom.

Mantra (Sanskrit; *ngag* Tibetan) The word mantra is an abbreviation of two syllables *mana* and *tara*, respectively meaning 'mind' and 'protection:' coming from the mind, giving protection through transformation. Mantras are Sanskrit words or syllables that express the quintessence of particular energies or of a deity. They protect the mind from distraction and serve as support for meditation. Mantras can be sung or spoken out loud, quietly recited 'just loud enough for your collar to hear' or recited silently.

Naropa (1016-1100) was a great Indian scholar, chief disciple of Tilopa and guru to Marpa; these are the forefathers of the Kagyu lineage.

Ngöndro (Tibetan) is a series of practices comprising Four Ordinary Foundations and Four Extraordinary Foundations. They were originally created for the Tibetan people by the Indian Mahasiddha, Atisha Dipamkara and are treated as the gateway to all deep Vajrayana practices. The Ordinary Foundations are contemplations on: precious human birth, death and impermanence, karma and samsara. The Four Extraordinary Foundations are the recitation of: 100,000 refuge prayers and prostrations, 100,000 Vajrasattva mantras, 100,000 mandala offerings, and 100,000 guru yoga practices. The Ngöndro is practised by all schools of Tibetan Buddhism with slight variations. See *The Ngöndro: Foundation Practices of Mahamudra* by Ringu Tulku Rinpoche: Bodhicharya Publications 2013.

Nirvana (Sanskrit; *nyangde* Tibetan) literally means 'extinguished' and is the state of being free from all suffering. It is the opposite of samsara and arises when we have completely done away with all the obscurations, misunderstandings, negative emotions and other hindrances that create samsaric existence. When we are free from all fear and suffering and our mind is completely clear; this is described as enlightenment or nirvana.

Padmasambhava see *Guru Padmasambhava.*

Pandit (Sanskrit) means a great scholar or philosopher.

Patrul Rinpoche (1808 - 1887) was an outstanding master of Tibetan Buddhism of the 19th century. He was a great scholar and Dzogchen master who wrote the *Words of My Perfect Teacher,* a classic for the Nyingma school. Some of the most important living Dzogchen and Mahamudra lineage teachings today, came from Patrul Rinpoche.

Phowa (Tibetan) is a meditation practice of 'transferring the consciousness at the time of death.'

Pranayama (Sanskrit) means extension of the breath or subtle energy; an aspect of yoga training, for example Hatha Yoga, which focuses on breathing exercises that stimulate the flow of subtle energy.

Sadhana (*drub tab* Tibetan), literally 'means of accomplishment,' refers to the text of a ritual practice that may be followed by a practitioner who has been initiated into it.

A typical sadhana structure usually starts with taking refuge and arousing Bodhicitta. The main part of the practice involves visualisation and mantra recitation and the sadhana concludes by dedicating the merit of the practice to all sentient beings.

Sakya Pandita (*Drogmé Lotsawa*) (1182 - 1251 AD) was a scholar and founder of the Sakya Order, one of the four main schools of Tibetan Buddhism.

Samadhi (Sanskrit; *ting nge zin* Tibetan) is a state of meditative absorption in which the mind rests unwaveringly.

Samsara (Sanskrit; *khor wa* Tibetan) is the state of suffering of 'cyclical existence.' It describes a state of mind that experiences gross and / or subtle pain and dissatisfaction. It arises because the mind is deluded and unclear and thus perpetually conditioned by attachment, aversion and ignorance.

Shamatha (Sanskrit; *shiné / shinay* Tibetan) is calm abiding meditation: calming and stabilising the mind to bring it to a state of peace. Sometimes also called tranquillity meditation.

Shantarakshita (Sanskrit; *Shiwa Tso* Tibetan) (725–788) was a great Indian pandit and abbot of Nalanda monastic college. He was invited to Tibet by King Trisong Detsen, where he founded Samye monastery and ordained the first Tibetan monks.

Six Paramitas (Sanskrit; *Parami* Pali) are literally the *perfections* which together lay out the path of practice for a Bodhisattva. Generosity is paramount and comes first, the others unfolding one by one from the other, to give the six: Generosity, Morality (Good Conduct or Discipline), Patience, Diligence, Meditation and Wisdom. Wisdom is both the fruition of the other Paramitas and informs the practice of them all.

Sravakayana (Sanskrit), literally 'the vehicle of the hearers and listeners,' is the foundational vehicle of Buddhism. It follows the common teachings of the Buddha, which are accepted by all the Buddhist vehicles. The Sravakayana covers the commonly used term Hinayana (or 'small vehicle'), and is in effect equivalent to Theravada Buddhism, in the modern world, combined with the Pratyekabuddhayana (or 'vehicle of the solitary realisers'). The emphasis of these paths is on personal liberation from the suffering of samsara.

Sugata (Sanskrit; *dewar shekpa* Tibetan) is 'one thus gone to bliss,' similar to

Tathagata but with more emphasis on the blissful nature of full realisation or enlightenment (Tathagata emphasising more the wisdom aspect).

Sutrayana (Sanskrit) is the vehicle of the Buddha's teachings following the sutras (*do* in Tibetan): the teachings given by Shakyamuni Buddha, memorised by his disciples and subsequently written down. These are often contrasted with the tantras, which are the Buddha's Vajrayana teachings and the shastras, which are commentaries on the words of the Buddha.

Tathagata (Sanskrit) is the name the Buddha used to refer to himself in the Sutras. It means the 'one thus gone' (and also 'one thus come') and is an epithet for a fully realised Buddha.

Terma or 'treasure findings' are concealed teachings, which were hidden by great Bodhisattvas and then revealed or discovered at a later time by a *terton*, or 'treasure finder.' Guru Rinpoche and Yeshe Tsogyal hid many such teachings, for example, for the benefit of future disciples. Terma may be actual physical texts, sometimes found in rocks or similar natural places, or they may come as direct mind transmissions.

Theravada (Pali; *ne ten de pa* Tibetan) is a school of Buddhism, which follows the sutras in Pali. Sometimes called 'the way of the elders,' they follow the Sravakayana, which is the vehicle of the common or foundational teachings of the Buddha. (The Sravakayana and Theravada Buddhism are almost synonymous in practicality because most of the other schools that followed the Sravakayana teachings no longer exist.) See also *Sravakayana*.

Tonglen (Tibetan) is a meditation practice of [literally] 'sending and taking:' sending out healing love and positivity, and taking upon one's self the sufferings and pain of the world. The visualisation works to uproot ego clinging and fear and instead generate Bodhicitta.

Tsa lung (Tibetan; *nadi prana* Sanskrit), as a pair of terms, refer to the subtle channels *(tsa)* of the body and the wind *(lung)* or subtle energy that flows through them. Usually meaning breathing exercises that stimulate this flow of subtle energy.

Tummo (Tibetan; *chandali* Sanskrit) literally means 'fierce woman' and describes inner heat generated through specific meditation techniques; the first of the Six Doctrines of Naropa.

Vajra (Sanskrit; *dorje* Tibetan) is sometimes translated as 'diamond-like.' It symbolises that which is indestructible, that which can cut through anything else but cannot, itself, be destroyed. The symbol is a ritual object like a kind of sceptre, made of metal. What it symbolises is the vajra state, attained through understanding the essence of mind as pure emptiness. Once this understanding is attained, we know there is nothing that can be destroyed because everything exists in emptiness. So, we realise we are indestructible in this way and this is ultimately what frees us from all fear and clinging.

Vajradhara (Sanskrit; *Dorje Chang* Tibetan), literally, 'Holder of the Varja,' is the indestructible and primordial Buddha. He is blue, the colour of deep space, depicting the true nature of our mind: changeless, timeless and unlimited. He holds a bell and a vajra in his hands, crossed in the union mudra, representing the union of wisdom and compassion.

Vajrakilaya is the wrathful form of Vajrasattva. See also *wrathful deities*.

Vajrayana Buddhism (Sanskrit; *dorje tek pa* Tibetan) *Vajra* means 'diamond-like' or of 'indestructible capacity,' conveying a sense of what is beyond arising and ceasing, and is therefore indestructible. The Vajrayana is the third vehicle of Buddhism and provides a path of compassionate wisdom that sees through all illusion. It incorporates and accepts all the teachings of the Sravakayana and the Bodhisattvayana (or Mahayana) and then also includes teachings on the tantras and various skilful means. It elaborates on the concept of Buddhanature and uses the method of taking the result as the path. It may afford the practitioner swift progress, practised in accordance with the foundations of Buddhist approach. See also *Mahayana, Sravakayana*.

Vimalamitra (Sanskrit; *Drimay Shenyen* Tibetan) was a great Indian master, who went to Tibet in the 9th century, where he taught, composed and translated many Sanskrit Buddhist texts.

Vipashyana (Sanskrit; *vipassana* Pali; *lhakthong* Tibetan) means 'Insight Meditation.' It is usually practised after gaining some experience of 'calm-abiding' meditation and refers to gaining insight into your true nature, seeing yourself truly and directly, which becomes the basis for transformation. See also *Shamatha*.

Wrathful Deities see *Deity*; wrathful deities particularly embody the aspect of power of enlightened mind: power and might expressed with wisdom and compassion, to subdue and cut through strong emotions or negative views.

Yidam (Tibetan; *istadevata* Sanskrit), is literally a shortened version of the meaning 'samaya of mind.' It refers to a personification or archetype of specific enlightened qualities that a practitioner takes as their inspiration, in order to develop such qualities themselves. See also *Deity*.

Yoga (Sanskrit; *naljor* Tibetan) comes from the Sanskrit meaning 'to yoke' together. In a Buddhist context it usually means joining or uniting with the natural state of mind. Also used more generally to refer to physical exercises, which bring mind and body together, such as those in the Indian yoga tradition; for example, Hatha Yoga.

Yogi (Sanskrit; *naljorpa* Tibetan), or **yogini**, feminine; is someone who has stable recognition of the natural state of mind. Also used more generally to mean a Vajrayana practitioner or any practitioner whose emphasis is on experiential understanding and integrating that with one's life and being, as opposed to purely intellectual or scholarly understanding.

Notes

1. Ringu Tulku's own 'loose translation' of a traditional Tibetan saying.
2. From the Ngöndro translation, by Katia Holmes, with guidance from Khenchen Thrangu Rinpoche, 1980 © Kagyu Samye Ling.
3. From *'The Dhammapada, The Sayings of the Buddha.' Chapter 12: 'Yourself.'* Published by Rider Books: 2008 edition. Translated by Thomas Byrom.
4. Calligraphies of these long and short mantras, in Tibetan, Uchen script, by Tashi Mannox, may be found on page 107 (six syllable mantra) and page 105 (hundred syllable mantra).

Editor's Note: Throughout the Heart Wisdom series we have used the word *student* to identify questions and discussion from audience members. This is not intended to imply the speaker would necessarily identify themselves as students of Tibetan Buddhism or of Ringu Tulku. It refers to the fact that they are being a 'student,' just in this instance, by virtue of asking a question in order to understand more.

Acknowledgements

Immense thanks go to everyone who contributed to the retreat, on which this book is based, at Bodhicharya Meditation Centre in Sikkim, India. Particularly to mention Erika van Greunen, the organiser, whose hard work and expertise in this yielded a wonderful retreat, which we all benefitted from. And Pema Namgyal, Rinpoche's brother, who assisted without reserve in every way possible. It was gratitude for this chance we had, that encouraged me to write up the teachings, so they could spread further afield and this blessing be shared with others. Thank you to Bernie Vorster for supplying the recordings of the teachings from this retreat, which we worked from to produce the book.

Gratitude also goes to the many people who work on these books to bring them to fruition: to Rachel Moffitt who oversees the administrative side of Bodhicharya Publications, from printing books through to distributing them. To Paul O'Connor who brings each book alive through providing the layout and design. To Mariette van Lieshout who proofread the final drafts of this text. To Anna Howard who offered comments. To Lama Wangmo who checked the Tibetan and Sanskrit terms for us. And to Martin Hird who provided some of the new terms for the glossary. Thank you to all the Dharma centres that have supported the work of writing up this book, by providing suitable environments in which to concentrate on it wholeheartedly. Particularly, I would like to thank Sonia Moriceau and Ad Brugman for welcoming me at their Dharma centre, The Orchard, over the years; which enabled much of the writing up of this book.

Thank you to His Holiness the 17th Karmapa for writing, and giving us permission to use and reprint here, his concise text on the Four Preliminary Practices. Thank you also to the artists that created beautiful and precious designs, and gave them freely for publication here: to Salga for the image of Vajrasattva and to Tashi Mannox for his calligraphies of the Vajrasattva mantras. Thank you to Paul O'Connor for his inspired depiction of the mantra garland encircling the HUNG, and to those who advised us on how it should look.

A bow of acknowledgement and well wishing, also, to all fellow students on this path. These books are written for you, and they are shaped by you, too. From the organisers of teachings, through to those attending and asking questions, to those of us who work on creating books from the teachings - and all the conversations and learnings we share along the way - there are many seen and unseen influences on how these books take form.

All of our heartfelt thanks go to our teacher, Ringu Tulku, who always seems to find exactly the right words to guide us - if only we will listen. Thank you Rinpoche for learning so deeply and comprehensively the English language, and for listening so patiently to the 'ways of Westerners.' Thank you for talking to us where we are at, and so providing a bridge for us to meet the profundity of these teachings.

Mary Dechen Jinpa
On behalf of Bodhicharya Publications
Oxford, November 2015

About the Author

Ringu Tulku Rinpoche is a Tibetan Buddhist Master of the Kagyu Order. He was trained in all schools of Tibetan Buddhism under many great masters including HH the 16th Gyalwang Karmapa and HH Dilgo Khyentse Rinpoche. He took his formal education at Namgyal Institute of Tibetology, Sikkim and Sampurnananda Sanskrit University, Varanasi, India. He served as Tibetan Textbook Writer and Professor of Tibetan Studies in Sikkim for 25 years.

Since 1990, he has been travelling and teaching Buddhism and meditation in Europe, America, Canada, Australia and Asia. He participates in various interfaith and 'Science and Buddhism' dialogues and is the author of several books on Buddhist topics. These include *Path to Buddhahood, Daring Steps, The Ri-me Philosophy of Jamgon Kongtrul the Great, Confusion Arises as Wisdom*, the *Lazy Lama* series and the *Heart Wisdom* series, as well as several children's books, available in Tibetan and European languages.

He founded the organisations Bodhicharya - see www.bodhicharya.org and Rigul Trust - see www.rigultrust.org.

For an up to date list of books by Ringu Tulku, please see the Books section at

www.bodhicharya.org

Our professional skills are given free of charge in order to produce these books, and Bodhicharya Publications is run by volunteers; so your purchase of this book goes entirely to fund further books and contribute to humanitarian and educational projects supported by Bodhicharya.

Thank you.

The Ringu Tulku Archive
THE RECORDED TEACHINGS OF RINGU TULKU RINPOCHE

www.bodhicharya.org/teachings